100 WALKS IN
Surrey

compiled by

CLIVE SCOTT

The Crowood Press

First published in 1994 by
The Crowood Press Ltd
Ramsbury
Marlborough
Wiltshire SN8 2HR

This impression 1997

© The Crowood Press Ltd 1994

British Library Cataloguing-in-Publication Data
A catalogue record for this book is
available from the British Libary

ISBN 1 85223 806 2

All maps by Janet Powell

Typeset by Carreg Limited, Ross-on-Wye, Herefordshire

Printed in Great Britain by Redwood Books, Trowbridge, Wiltshire

CONTENTS

PUBLISHER'S NOTE

We very much hope that you enjoy the routes presented in this book, which has been compiled with the aim of allowing you to explore the area in the best possible way – on foot.

We strongly recommend that you take the relevant map for the area, and for this reason we list the appropriate Ordnance Survey maps for each route. Whilst the details and descriptions given for each walk were accurate at time of writing, the countryside is constantly changing, and a map will be essential if, for any reason, you are unable to follow the given route. It is good practice to carry a map and use it so that you are always aware of your exact location.

We cannot be held responsible if some of the details in the route descriptions are found to be inaccurate, but should be grateful if walkers would advise us of any major alterations. Please note that whenever you are walking in the countryside you are on somebody else's land, and we must stress that you should *always* keep to established rights of way, and *never* cross fences, hedges or other boundaries unless there is a clear crossing point.

Remember the country code:

Enjoy the country and respect its life and work
Guard against all risk of fire
Fasten all gates
Keep dogs under close control
Keep to public footpaths across all farmland
Use gates and stiles to cross field boundaries
Leave all livestock, machinery and crops alone
Take your litter home
Help to keep all water clean
Protect wildlife, plants and trees
Make no unnecessary noise

The walks are listed by length – from approximately 1 to 12 miles – but the amount of time taken will depend on the fitness of the walkers and the time spent exploring any points of interest along the way. Nearly all the walks are circular and most offer recommendations for refreshments.

Good walking.

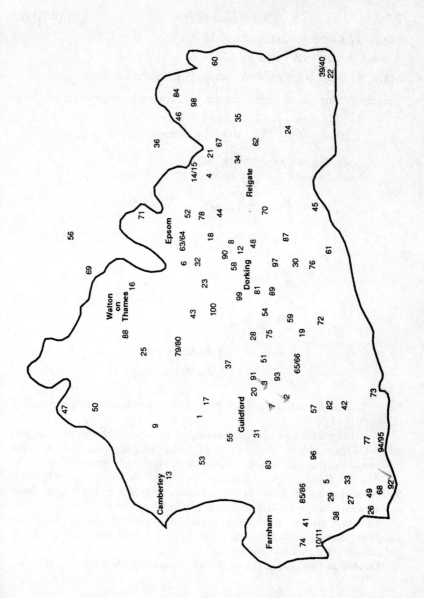

Walk 1   SEND CHURCH   2³/₄m (4¹/₂km)

Maps: OS Sheets Landranger 186; Pathfinder 1206.
A walk beside river and canal.
Start: At 018560, the New Inn, Cartbridge, Send.

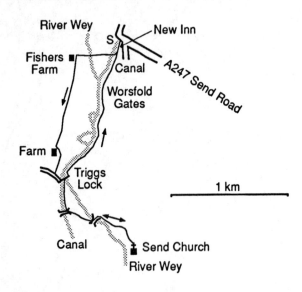

Note: This walk is not recommended after prolonged rain because of the possibility of waterlogged ground.

Both this and the walk to Papercourt Lock (Walk 17) start from the New Inn, and follow the River Wey and the Navigation Canal. Even in dry weather, some of the water meadows may well be wet, so stout footwear is strongly advised.

The Wey Navigation runs beside the New Inn; follow the gravel drive beside it for 100 yards, going south from the Inn, and cross a footbridge. Follow the path ahead to reach a drive and continue, to cross two branches of the river.

In front of Fishers Farm, turn left and follow a track to the entrance to another farm. Turn left over a stile and follow the ditch round to reach another stile. Go over and turn left along a track to Triggs Lock.

Go over the lock gates and turn right along the towpath towards the bridge ahead.

There, turn left, away from the canal, through a metal gate, aiming directly for **Send church**. It is this area that could well be flooded. If it is then you may have to postpone your visit to the church.

If conditions permit, go across the watermeadow and over the footbridge. Skirt a farmhouse and continue to reach the church. It is curious to note that no village exists in the immediate vicinity!

To return, retrace the route to Triggs Lock and go over the footbridge at the point where river and canal join. Now follow the river bank to reach **Worsfold Gates** where the river and canal diverge. There, follow the towpath back to the start.

POINTS OF INTEREST:

Send Church – A church has stood on the site presently occupied by St Mary the Virgin, Send for over 900 years, one being mentioned in the Domesday Survey of 1086.

Worsfold Gates – The gates form a lock which is normally left open, but can be closed in times of flood. The gates are equipped with hand-drawn paddles, and the sluices are opened by pulling them up and inserting a peg to hold them open.

REFRESHMENTS:

The New Inn, Cartbridge, at the start of the walk.

Walk 2   CHINTHURST HILL $2^3/_4$m ($4^1/_2$km)

Maps: OS Sheets Landranger 186; Pathfinder 1226.

A fairly easy ascent through larch and chestnut with a rewarding view.

Start: At 017452, the Grantley Arms Inn, Wonersh.

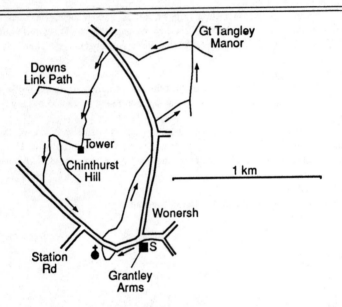

From the inn, go along The Street towards Bramley, as indicated above the tile-covered seat shelter. Very soon the church tower comes into view. Just beyond the drive to Wonersh House (private), turn left through the archway, crossing the green to enter the churchyard of St John the Baptist up five steps. Bear right around the wall to return to the road. Turn left for 50 yards, then go right along the footpath beyond the wall of Green Place.

    Keep ahead through a gate, passing the bowling green to the right. The path joins a gravel drive: follow it to a road. Turn left and, about 75 yards past the junction with Blackheath Lane, bear right to reach a footpath through a gap in the wall beside the entrance to Little Tangley. This path joins a stony track which goes around a double bend towards a nursery. Opposite the Old Coach House, turn left at a finger post. At this point, St Martha's Church is visible on top of the hill ahead just to the right.

At the end of the field, there is a cluster of buildings around Great Tangley Manor. Turn left here, going along the Downs Link Path. Look out for the clear right fork and follow it to a road. Cross with care, and pass the side of the red-tile-roofed Falcon Cottage.

At a junction, keep ahead, following a finger-post to the **tower**. The ascent under the trees is assisted by steps and zig-zags: there is even a seat placed at a crossing track on which to regain your breath before the final push to the summit! At the top, there is not only the tower, but a rewarding view and plenty of room to sit, relax, and maybe enjoy a picnic.

In your own time, return to the seat at the crossing, and now turn left along the track. Walk to a wooden barrier, beyond which you join a surfaced drive and descend to a road. Turn left here and keep ahead at the junction to return to **Wonersh** and the Grantley Arms.

POINTS OF INTEREST:

Tower – The tower on top of Chinthurst Hill is an 18th century folly. The grassland around it provides an excellent picnic spot and a place to enjoy the good view, notwithstanding a height of just less than 400 feet.

Wonersh – The village lies in the valley between the Barnett and Chinthurst Hills. It won the best-kept Surrey village award in 1970, 1976 and 1980.

The secluded church green, as the notice in the entrance archway dated November 1936 tells you, is 'open by permission of the owner until further notice for the quiet use of the residents of Wonersh'. In 1950, the tablet opposite states, it was placed in perpetual trust for the same purpose. The frieze on both walls was the work of a local resident, John Hurren. It was completed in 1953 and has a text from Isaiah, chapter 41, verse 6: 'They helped every one his neighbour; and every one said to his brother, Be of good courage'.

REFRESHMENTS:

The Grantley Arms Inn, Wonersh.

Walk 3 SHALFORD AND ST CATHERINE'S CHAPEL 2³/₄m (4¹/₂km)

Maps: OS Sheets Landranger 186; Pathfinder 1226 and 1225.

Enjoy the charm of a stroll alongside the River Wey.

Start: At 000477, the Sea Horse Inn, Shalford.

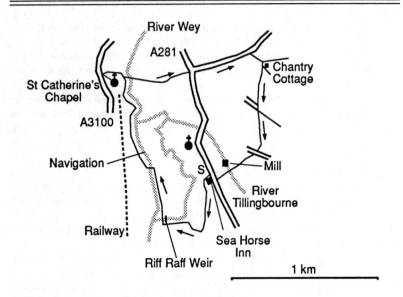

Beyond the wall of the Sea Horse Inn's car park, turn left along the bridleway. This bears left, passing the rear gardens of some houses. At the top, go right, through a gateway, and drop down to the water meadows of the River Wey. Keep ahead over the walkway and go along the bank to reach the Riff Raff weir.

Go around the cottage, perhaps sharing the view with those in a passing train or on a canal boat. Cross to the other bank at the lock and continue along the towpath, with **St Catherine's Chapel** jutting into the sky ahead. At the footbridge, you can either clamber steeply up the hill to have a look at the ruins, or else use the lane a few yards further on by the stone seat and miniature bridge.

To continue the walk, go over the footbridge and head away from the river. Cross a playing field and, at the main road, continue ahead along Pilgrims Way. At the bend opposite the Echo Pit Road nameboard, bear right, following the Guildford

Nature Trail and North Downs Way finger-posts. Soon you will reach **Chantry Cottage** situated at the entrance to Chantry Woods. Turn right on to the sandy footpath and follow it to reach a residential road. Keep ahead on this, then continue on the footpath running alongside. Cross the road at the bottom, go up the steps opposite and cross the field beyond. Very shortly you will reach **Shalford Mill**: the Sea Horse Inn, the start of the walk, is just beyond.

POINTS OF INTEREST:
St Catherine's Chapel – The chapel, dating from the 14th century, is now a ruin. It lies on the route of the old Pilgrims' Way that ran from Winchester to Canterbury.
Chantry Cottage – The Chantries, or Chantry Woods, got their name from the chantry set up in 1486 by a man named Henry Norbridge. In the Middle Ages a chantry was an endowment which paid for a priest to pray, or sing for souls of the dead. The name derives from the French *chanter*, to sing.

Today, the tree-covered sandy ridge close to the cottage that bears the old name is owned by Guildford Borough Council. It has a Nature Trail, for which a descriptive leaflet can be obtained from the Tourist Office in High Street, telephone 0483 444007.
Shalford Mill – The mill, which dates from the 18th century, sits astride the River Tillingbourne, a short distance from its confluence with the Wey. In use as a corn mill until 1914, it fell into disrepair, but was restored in the early 1930s through the efforts of a group of enthusiasts known as Ferguson's Gang. The machinery is largely intact today. The building is owned by the National Trust, and is open to the public.

REFRESHMENTS:
The Sea Horse Inn, at Shalford.

Walk 4   CHIPSTEAD   3m (4³/₄km)

Maps: OS Sheets Landranger 187; Pathfinder 1207.
An undulating walk along a secluded valley.
Start: At 278567, the car park behind Elmore Pond.

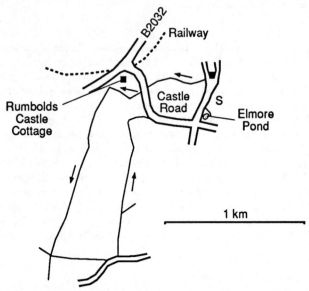

From the car park walk along High Road, going away from the crossroads to reach
the White Hart Inn. There, fork left and after a few yards take the grassy track going
left. This track leads to a barrier beyond which it descends beneath tree cover. Bear
left to reach a road (Castle Road). Cross and go over a stile in the hedgerow opposite.
Descend to reach the fenced electricity compound beside the road. Here, look over to
your right to see **Rumbolds Castle Cottage**, the house nestling under the railway
viaduct.

    Do not cross the stile out to the road; instead, double back, heading up the grassy
hillside dotted with trees and bushes to reach a stile. Cross and walk through a narrow
belt of trees. Beyond the trees, turn right around a large sloping field. About 50 yards
along the top side, go up right, through a gap to reach a footpath. Turn left along this
broad path.

Stay with the path, keeping ahead at a path crossing and bearing right at a later fork. When a house, Pigeonhouse Farm, comes into view ahead, turn left and descend to reach a road. Follow the road uphill for a few yards to reach a stile on the left. Go over and follow the path beyond across a field to reach a track. Continue ahead on the track; you are now walking parallel to the outward route, but on the other side of the valley.

When a gate and stile are reached, turn up right to reach a road (Castle Road again). Do not go out on to the road; instead, turn right, staying inside the field going uphill to reach its top where you emerge close to the village pumphouse (which is now kept locked) of **Chipstead**. Turn left to reach the pond.

POINTS OF INTEREST:
Rumbolds Castle Cottage – The cottage dates from the 16th century, and was originally a public house.
Chipstead – The village name derives from the old words 'cheap'/'chipping' meaning a market.

REFRESHMENTS:
The White Hart, Chipstead.

Walk 5   **THURSLEY AND HOUNDOWN**   3m (4³/₄km)

Maps: OS Sheets Landranger 186; Pathfinder 1245 and 1225.

An easy walk on sandy tracks..

Start: At 902397, the Green in Thursley.

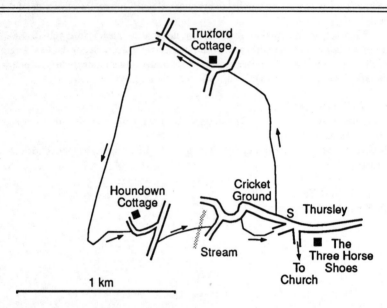

From the triangular green in Thursley, walk along the pavement past the telephone and letter boxes. Cross the grass by the children's play area to find a path below the cricket pitch. The path leads through trees and bracken to join a sandy bridleway running beside a field on the left. At a fork, bear left passing a green-painted barn to join a track leading to a road.

Turn left, and keep ahead at the next bend beside Truxford Cottage. When a crossing is reached, take the narrow path going half-left and uphill. Heather, pines and gorse have taken over the area now crossed by the route and a line of pylons. Bear left on the soft sand. Over to the right, but not yet visible from the track you are on, is a substantial depression. It is readily visible from a viewpoint at the top of a wide sandy gully. After enjoying the view descend into a dip. Here, as you look to the right, you could well have a sense of total seclusion from the outside world; no buildings, no vehicles, probably no other people.

Keep ahead up the rise and pass to the left side of a rounded hill. At a path junction, take the second turning left and then the left fork beyond the wooden post. Keep ahead at a pylon to reach a group of lofty conifers. Now drop down, joining other tracks that are all heading for the bridge over a stream.

Bear left up the lane beyond to reach a road. Go right for 100 yards to the reach the 'Slow' road marking. Here, turn left down a path. Go over a bridge and descend through a gully to reach a crystal-clear and fast-flowing stream, its banks providing a justifiably popular picnic spot. Turn left along the drive ahead to reach a road. Turn right up the road between the cottages and at the bend take the path going up the gully to the right. Keep ahead below a bank of bracken and continue to reach a lane. Now follow the lane past some charming cottages to reach the start.

POINTS OF INTEREST:
Thursley – The name is an adaptation of Thor's Lea, the god being represented on the sign sited in the triangle of green where the walk starts.

REFRESHMENTS:
The Three Horseshoes, Thursley.

Walk 6　　　　LEATHERHEAD COMMON　　　3m (4³/₄km)

Maps: OS Sheets Landranger 187; Pathfinder 1206.

A level walk, mainly through woodland.

Start: At 162583, the Tesco car park, off Kingston Road, Leatherhead.

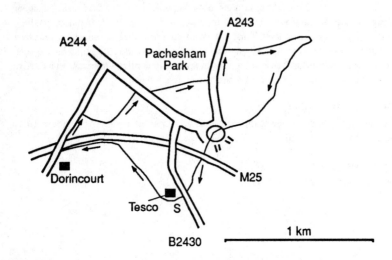

From the entrance to the Tesco car park, continue away from the roundabout to reach a bend. Here, take the paved path beside the black railings, going over a wooden footbridge. Turn right, following the LCW sign towards Oaklawn Road. The path ascends gently with Teazle Wood on the left, then descends to walk alongside the M25. Continue to reach a road bridge beside **Dorincourt**.

Cross the motorway and, after 50 yards, turn right and immediately left, following the green waymarking arrowheads. Turn into a wood opposite the entrance to Tyrwhitt House, following a path through it, crossing a couple of streams by way of plank bridges. At a T-junction of paths, turn left to reach a road. Go right for 50 yards, then turn between the stone pillars into Pachesham Park. Keep ahead to cross the golf course, continuing in the same direction beyond to reach a main road (the A243).

Cross with care, and turn left to reach double metal gates. Go right, and at the Corporation of London board, keep ahead to reach a broad clearing. The path bears off half-right at the far end, passing through an area being cleared of sycamore. Go right at a T-junction of paths, and right again along the fringe of woodland. Bear right at a fork, and follow the green waymarking arrows to emerge at a roundabout. Pass under this by means of two subways. Cross the M25 motorway again, and follow the road down to the roundabout close to the start.

POINTS OF INTEREST:
Dorincourt – This is a home run by Queen Elizabeth's Foundation for Disabled People.
Sycamore – This is a non-native tree, which is of a lower wildlife conservation value than many native trees, such as oak. It spreads easily by wind-borne seeds, and, if unchecked, would soon take over the woodland.

REFRESHMENTS:
The Royal Oak, Kingston Road, near start of the walk.

Walk 7 CHANTRY WOODS AND PEWLEY DOWN 3m (4³/₄km)

Maps: OS Sheets Landranger 186; Pathfinder 1226.

Fine views throughout, and an opportunity for further exploration along a Nature Trail.

Start: At 021484, Halfpenny Lane car park beside St Martha's Hill.

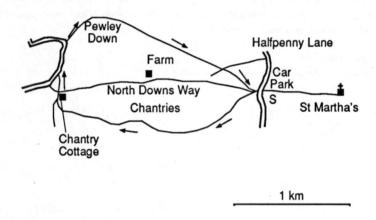

From the parking area at the western foot of St Martha's Hill, walk left along Halfpenny Lane to find the North Downs Way on your right. Go through the metal barrier and at once fork left. The path rises through woodland to reach a camp site on the left: skirt this to emerge on to open grassland with fine views.

At the end of the grass, with the green spire of St Mary's Church, Shalford ahead, join a path which descends, then rises using a log staircase. Beyond this, go gently downhill, passing two rustic seats facing a clearing on the left. **Guildford Cathedral** can soon be glimpsed half-right. The main path now curls right to reach an information board just above **Chantry Cottage**.

Go through the gate here, and turn right along the embankment above the car park to reach a road. Go right on the pavement up to the sharp bend, then keep ahead up Northdown Lane. When this bears right, stay outside the fence and ascend to the top of Pewley Down.

Turn right along the ridge, going past the commemorative pedestal, and then go down half-right by the hedgerow. Maintain this direction to the end of the fields, then go straight over a track by a red post to re-enter the woods. A short ascent now returns you to the road where the walk started.

POINTS OF INTEREST:

Guildford Cathedral – The cathedral which is seen, but not visited, during this walk was completed as recently as 1961. Construction of this, the first Anglican cathedral to be newly built since the Reformation, commenced in 1936 under the architect, Sir Edward Maufe.

Chantry Cottage – The Chantries, or Chantry Woods, got their name from the chantry set up in 1486 by a man named Henry Norbridge. In the Middle Ages a chantry was an endowment which paid for a priest to pray, or sing for souls of the dead. The name derives from the French *chanter*, to sing.

Today, the tree-covered sandy ridge close to the cottage that bears the old name is owned by Guildford Borough Council. It has a Nature Trail, for which a descriptive leaflet can be obtained from the Tourist Office in High Street, telephone 0483 444007.

REFRESHMENTS:

None en route, but there are possibilities in the local villages.

Walk 8   MICKLEHAM DOWNS   3m (4³/₄km)

Maps: OS Sheets Landranger 187; Pathfinder 1206.
A fine ridge of grassland.
Start: At 170534, the Running Horses Inn, Mickleham.

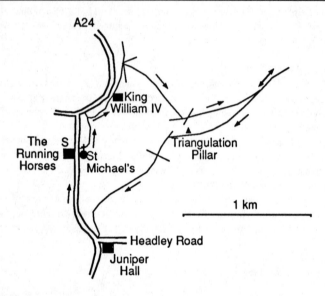

From the **Running Horses Inn**, go into St Michael's churchyard beside The Rectory and walk alongside the Lloyd memorial wall. Turn left at its end and continue over a drive to reach a junction by a cottage gate. Go right, continuing along the lane beyond Lammas Cottage to reach Byttom Hill near the A24.

Turn right to pass The King William IV Inn and climb steadily to reach a five-way junction. Take the steep path beyond the metal gate until you reach the second stile, then turn left to pick up the blue arrowheads again at post 8.

You come out on the open ridge of Mickleham Downs by post 9. The walk goes right here, but before doing so it is worth walking to the left, just be able to say that you have covered the entire length of grassland.

Back on the route, as you approach the other end, bear slightly to the right to spy the triangulation pillar tucked away in a corner. Do not take the path directly passing the pillar: instead, take the grass path ahead into the trees and, beyond the metal pole, turn left along a track and walk all the way down to reach a road opposite a house called **Juniper Hall**.

Turn right, and return to the village using the footpath behind the hedge.

POINTS OF INTEREST:

The Running Horses Inn – Although built much earlier, the inn gets its present name from the Derby of 1828, when there was a dead-heat between 'Cadland' and 'The Colonel'. Both horses are painted on one side of the inn sign, but only 'Cadland', the winner of the re-run, appears on the other side.

Juniper Hall – This should not be confused with the house opposite called Juniper Hill. The Hall is now a field study centre, but is not open to the public. In 1793, the house provided shelter for a group of French aristocrats who had fled to England to escape the post Revolution regime. One of these was General Alexandre d'Arblay, and it was here that he met the novelist and diarist, Fanny Burney (1752-1840). They were married in Mickleham church and set up home at nearby Norbury Park. The cottage they built, and lived in between 1797 and 1801, was named Camilla Cottage, since it was financed by the success of her novel, *Camilla*, published in 1796.

For part of this circuit, you are following The National Trust Long Walk, waymarked with blue arrow heads. This starts at the top of Boxhill, and a descriptive leaflet can be purchased from the Information Centre there.

REFRESHMENTS:
The Running Horses Inn, Mickleham.
The King William IV, Mickleham.

Walk 9   CHOBHAM $3^1/_4$m (5km)

Maps: OS Sheets Landranger 186; Pathfinder 1189.

A level walk, outward along the riverbank.

Start: At 974619, the car park off Chobham High Street.

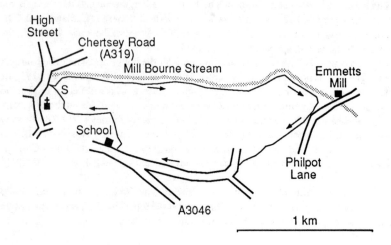

From the car park situated near the War Memorial and cannon, take the path that leads between a hedge and a fence, and bear left to the Mill Bourne stream. Walk along the riverbank path for $1^1/_2$ miles, finally emerging on to a road (Philpot Lane) beside Frogs Leap Farm. From this point take a small detour to the left, going along the road as far as the hump-back bridge in order to enjoy the sight of the stream cascading around the small island at Emmetts Mill.

Return to the point at which you emerged on to the road and walk past Frogs Leap Farm to reach the path on the far side of the grass frontage, beside the small clump of trees. At the far side, pass through a squeezer; the path continues beyond the tennis court, going to the right of a line of small conifers.

Beyond a brick wall, enter a paddock and aim for the thatched house, Imley Cottage, visible ahead, to reach a road. Now keep ahead on the road, walking down

24

past Chobham Farm to reach a junction with the main road. Stay on the right side of the road, and turn right along the path beside Flexlands School. Go past the tennis court and cross a plank bridge and stile. Cross the meadow beyond and, at the far side, find a stile just to the left. Go over the stile and turn left, heading for St Lawrence's Church. At the junction in front of the fenced cricket field, turn right to return directly to the car park.

POINTS OF INTEREST:
Nearby Fairoaks Airport accounts for the light aircraft activity which you are likely to witness through the walk.

REFRESHMENTS:
The Sun Inn, Chobham.

Walks 10 & 11   Frensham and Batts Corner $3\frac{1}{4}$m (5km) or $4\frac{1}{2}$m (7km)

Maps: OS Sheets Landranger 186; Pathfinder 1225.

A walk offering aspects of the River Wey, and, on the longer route, views across the Great Pond.

Start: At 842414, St Mary the Virgin Church, Frensham.

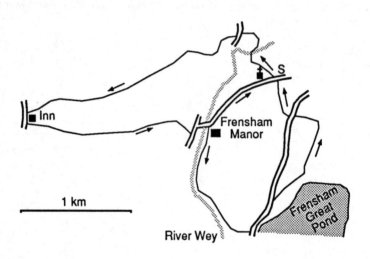

From the church, go down the footpath outside the church wall, and, after about five minutes walking, cross the River Wey on a wooden bridge. Continue up the path beyond, and go left along the lane at the top, passing The Malt House, to reach a road. Go straight across and up a drive, veering right opposite 'Sandpipers'. Go through a gate and, a few yards later, cross a stile. Bear left on a path along the edge of a field to enter a small wood. On emerging from the wood, keep ahead, walking with trees to the right. After about 100 yards, look for a stile in the hedgerow. Go over into the woodland, ascending to reach a track running along the top side of a sloping field.

Continue ahead to reach more woodland. When the field on the left ends, fork half-right along a grassy track which becomes a path. Eventually the path leads to a house (a kennels). Near this, cross into the adjacent field and walk in front of the building to join a drive which leads to a road. Turn left to reach the green and the Blue Bell inn at Batts Corner.

Go down the lane beside the pub's garden to join a track by Keepers Cottage. The tarmac surface soon restarts; continue to reach a fork beyond the Old Cottage/ Southfield. Go left to join a bridleway which leads to a road. Turn left to reach a junction by a white house, seemingly short of windows, and bear right to reach the River Wey as it pours away from a mill.

From this point the short walk continues along the road to return to the church.

For the longer walk, go through the gates of The Mill House, and take the track outside the wall beyond the wooden posts. Now follow the river, passing a new footbridge and skirting the grounds of Frensham Manor, on your left. The sound of rushing water draws your attention to a tranquil lake on the right a little distance after the river has swung away; carry on along the asphalt path to reach a road, with **Frensham Great Pond** in front of you, and a hotel a short distance to the right.

Turn left along the road (Bacon Lane) to reach a track which continues around the water's edge. Walk along the shore to reach a car parking area, then make for the chalet which houses toilets, a snack bar and the ranger's office. Go towards the Country Park entrance gate, but turn right along the bridleway just before the green barriers. After a slight ascent, a broad crossing is reached; turn up left. At the fire beater stop and look back at the Pond.

Now continue to the hill crest, then bear right and cross a broad track to find a narrow path leading down to a road. Turn left for 25 yards, then go right down a footpath to return to the church.

POINTS OF INTEREST:
Frensham Great Pond – The Pond is a popular sailing venue, and forms part of the Country Park.

REFRESHMENTS:
The Blue Bell Inn, Batts Corner.

Walk 12　　　　　　BOXHILL　　　　　$3\frac{1}{4}$m (5km)

Maps: OS Sheets Landranger 187; Pathfinder 1206.

A walk to Surrey's most visited beauty spot, though not the highest!

Start: At 178513, the National Trust Shop at top of Boxhill.

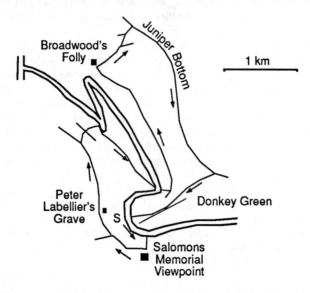

Boxhill is popular; almost a million people come each year! However, the great majority explore no further than the upper slopes around the **viewing platform**. You will, therefore, find peace and quiet, as well as some inviting picnic spots, particularly just before the tower, and in Happy Valley.

The route covered here follows for a large part, two walks described in separate National Trust leaflets, *The Short Walk* – orange leaflet – and *Nature Walk* – grey leaflet. You are recommended to buy both of these, for the invaluable nature notes they provide, before commencing the walk. The routes are indicated on the circuit by red and black arrowheads respectively. A further, longer, trail is waymarked in blue.

Leaving the shop and information centre, turn right to the road and continue beside this to reach the viewpoint. Take the path at the foot of the steps, walking in the direction of Hindhead. This is a section of the North Downs Way, marked with the acorn logo. Just beyond the end of the grass slope, the Way goes down to the left, but your route follows the red arrowhead, curling clockwise, with Denbies Vineyard covering the hillside opposite and the spire of Ranmore church piercing the sky beyond.

A stone placed in the middle of the path marks the grave of **Major Peter Labellière**. Beyond this, the walk commences a gradual descent on a chalky and uneven path. Look out for a post further down, almost at the point where the chalk regains a mantle of grass, which guides you to the right. After crossing a track, go down a long flight of steps, constructed in 1981 by volunteers, to reach a point just above the zig-zag road.

Turn right to the hair-pin bend and walk up the grassy floor of the valley. A short distance after crossing the road higher up, fork left to reach marker post Number 2 on the black arrowhead *Nature Walk*.

Bear left to reach the tower, then turn right along the obvious path. At the next fork, follow the blue *Long Walk* arrowheads down into Juniper Bottom. At a crossing, turn right and ascend through Happy Valley to reach post Number 14 at the top. At post Number 12, however, take a look at the yew, thought to be over 250 years old.

At the top, turn right for a level return to the start, going via the Donkey Green, the site of the National Trust's Country Day each summer.

POINTS OF INTEREST:
Viewing platform – The platform, situated at 564 feet (172 metres), overlooks Dorking and Brockham. It commemorates the gift of Boxhill to the nation in 1914 by Leopold Salomons, who lived in Norbury Park. The Park's cream-coloured mansion, seen on the top of the hill across the Mole valley, is viewed more closely on the Walk 58.

Major Peter Labellière – The Major was an eccentric resident of Dorking. He requested that, on his death, he should be buried head downwards. This duly took place on 11 July 1800, after he had died at the age of 75.

Tower – The tower, from which you look down to the Juniper Hall Field Centre, is named Broadwood's Folly. It was built by the piano maker, Thomas Broadwood, who purchased Juniper Hall in 1814.

REFRESHMENTS:
There is a café at the start of the walk.

Walk 13   AROUND PIRBRIGHT $3^1/_4$m ($5^1/_4$km)

Maps: OS Sheets Landranger 186; Pathfinder 1205.

A level circuit which could be combined with Walk 53 (Basingstoke Canal and Brookwood).

Start: At 946559, Pirbright Green pond.

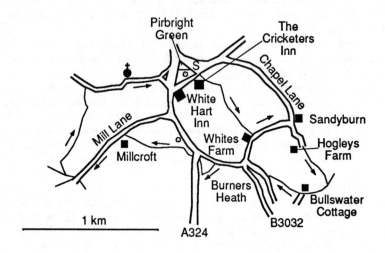

Take the path running between the Cricketers Inn and 'Myrtle Cottage' to pass through a white gate. At the end of the tarmac path, keep ahead on the gravel path for 20 yards, then turn right to pass some greenhouses. At the end of a straight pathway through the plantations of trees, go forward into a wood.

At the other end of the wood, cross a plank bridge and stile, and then head half-right across a field to reach Whites Farm. Turn left along the drive past the tennis court, and then bear right to meet a lane at 'Sandyburn'. Turn right and walk to 'Hogleys House'. Now follow the path ahead to the immediate left of the building. Cross the drive at the entrance to Hogleys Farm and continue forward, passing behind the garages of 'Heath Farm House'. A pleasant section of walking follows, going between the heather covered common and woodland to reach a junction. Turn right and cross the wooden footbridge over a stream to reach a path that goes beside a garden.

At the gravel drive to 'Bullswater Cottage', go forward for 50 yards and then turn right beyond 'Heather Lodge' to go along the drive to 'Springbok' and 'The Glade'. The alley beyond leads to the main road: walk along the pavement, going past Fords Farm and on to Burners Farm. Now cross the road, with care, and go through a barrier. Walk across a part of Burners Heath to reach the A324 and turn right along the wide grass verge to a road junction.

By the oak tree at the pond, go along the drive towards 'Cramond House', but fork right just inside the trees on to a path that ascends under laurels to emerge beside a paddock. Cross grassland and stiles to reach a lane. Turn left, walking past 'Millcroft' and Manor Farm, and continuing to go past the memorial seat to Mr G A G Smith. When the surfacing ends, go ahead past a car parking area and then bear right towards 'Brambles'. However, stay beside an old fence and climb a path above the drive to reach a field. Keep to the top side of the field, then descend beyond the far stile to cross a meadow. The path beyond crosses a stream and joins a road. Turn right, and, just past the 'No Entry' sign, use a field path on the right to rejoin the road at the church. Now continue along the lane back to **Pirbright Green**.

POINTS OF INTEREST:
Pirbright Green – The name Pirbright comes from *Perifrith*, a corruption of two old words meaning 'pear tree' and 'wood'. The wrought-iron sign on the Green, bearing both names, was erected to commemorate the Queen's Silver Jubilee in 1977.

REFRESHMENTS:
The Cricketers Inn, Pirbright.
The White Hart, Pirbright.
The Shop on the Green, Pirbright. Coffees and teas daily except Sunday.

Walks 14 & 15 BANSTEAD WOOD AND KINGSWOOD $3\frac{1}{2}$m ($5\frac{1}{2}$km)
or $5\frac{1}{4}$m ($8\frac{1}{2}$km)

Maps: OS Sheets Landranger 187; Pathfinder 1207.

An easy walk through wood and farmland, with pleasant valley views.

Start: At 273583, the car park at foot of Holly Lane, Chipstead.

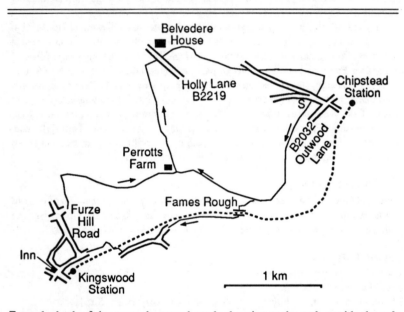

From the back of the car park, ascend gently, keeping to the path outside the pole fencing. The path climbs steadily under the trees and fine views are soon gained to the left, looking out across Chipstead Valley. You emerge from a canopy of trees to walk beside a cultivated field; continue over a broad crossing track to reach the end of the next field. Now take the path bearing right. After 200 yards, another path comes in acutely from the left, and 25 yards beyond, the short and long walks diverge beside a prominent yew tree.

The shorter walk continues ahead on the path for 250 yards to reach a T-junction. Here, turn left and stay on the wide path as it curves round to emerge from the wood high above the railway line running along the valley. At the stile, cross into grassland,

32

and keep to the right side to reach a brick barn at Perrotts Farm. Now rejoin the longer walk by taking the track ahead and slightly to the left.

The longer walk drops steeply down under the yew to emerge on to the secluded Fames Rough. Head for the lower side where, almost concealed from view, there is a railway arch. Go under this and turn right to enter an area run by the Woodland Trust. The bluebells hereabouts in May are truly spectacular.

At the far end, immediately past the second gate, turn left and then, after 25 yards, go right to reach a residential road. Veer right at the junction, and continue until the road rises. By number 37, 'Blantyre', take the signposted path down right. This leads across the railway track. On the other side of the track take the path going left and cross the car park to a driveway. The driveway joins St Monica's Road; go along this to a junction. The Kingswood Arms is to the left here.

Continue to the top of Furze Hill and turn left at the entrance to the new office complex. At the junction with Copt Hill Lane and Doric Drive, turn right for 100 yards on an unmade road, then go left along a footpath. The path leads to a farm track; turn right along this. In a few minutes you pass a couple of cottages on the left. Keep ahead as the track winds its way for half a mile to a farmhouse, where you rejoin the short walk.

Take the first footpath left after the walks rejoin, keeping on the wide track. Two gateways with stiles follow, after which you approach a wood and veer to the right to walk downhill beside a field. Keep ahead after one stile, cross another and turn right along a narrow path with low overhanging foliage. When a slip road is reached cross the main road immediately and take the footpath opposite, passing **Belvedere House** on the left. Skirt a field and cross a stile. Cross two broad tracks and a hundred yards beyond, veer left to cross a road. The path opposite goes downhill through woodland. At a fence at the bottom, turn right on a broad track which leads back down to the car park.

POINTS OF INTEREST:
Belvedere House – The house is now a retirement home run by the Royal Alfred Seafarers Society.

REFRESHMENTS:
The Kingswood Arms, Kingswood.

Walk 16 OXSHOTT HEATH AND ESHER COMMON 3$\frac{1}{2}$m (5$\frac{1}{2}$km)

Maps: OS Sheets Landranger 187; Pathfinder 1190.

A level walk mainly through woodland.

Start: At 142611, the car park at the approach to Oxshott Station.

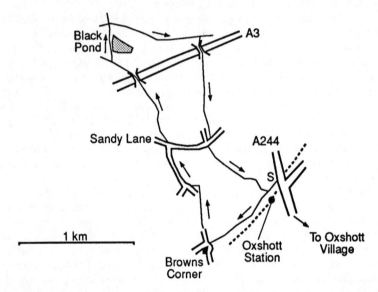

Follow the track out of the car park, going through the white barrier and continuing past the cottages. Take the path nearest to the railway and stay beside the lines, passing by a footbridge, to reach a road at **Brown's Corner**.

Turn along the path running parallel with the horse ride and heading in the direction of Sandy Lane. At a clearing, go through the barrier between the wooden fences to reach a road (The Ridings). Turn right. At the road end, follow the path going half-left beside Silver Greys. Go over the main A3 by way of West Bridge, turning left beyond, towards Portsmouth Road.

At a fork, go right through the wooden barrier to skirt Black Pond. At the next junction, take the right-hand path which leads into an avenue of pine trees. Join the horse ride to the Five Ways post in the clearing and keep ahead. The cindered track turns to sand before you reach a wide crossing. Now turn right, following the direction of the finger post, to Oxshott Heath. Re-cross the A3, this time by means of East Bridge, and drop down past a small pond with a seat for four.

Keep ahead to reach a road beside Roundhill Way. Go across and climb up the path immediately behind another finger post. Bear left, passing two marker posts for a circular walk, but continuing ahead at the second to reach the edge of a heather-clad slope.

Turn left to reach the War Memorial and then go down the broad steps. Bear left at the bottom to return to the car park.

POINTS OF INTEREST:
Brown's Corner – The memorial seat recalls the grocery and sweet shop run by members of the Brown family between 1907 and 1989. The building is no longer a shop but a private house.

REFRESHMENTS:
None en route, but *The Victoria Inn* can be found in Oxshott village, about half a mile from the start.

Walk 17   PAPERCOURT LOCK   3½m (5½km)

Maps: OS Sheets Landranger 186; Pathfinder 1206.

A walk beside river and canal, including a crossing of marshy ground.

Start: At 018560, the New Inn, Cartbridge, Send.

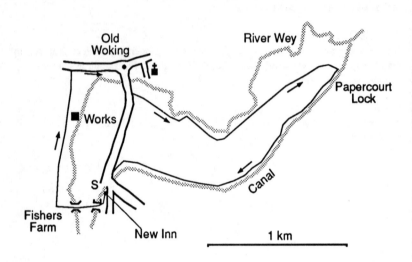

From the New Inn, follow the gravel drive along to the footbridge and cross both the canal and the branches of the Wey to reach Fishers Farm. Turn right and keep ahead along the edge of a field, passing through a copse and emerging beside a football pitch. Cross the bridge at the far end and turn left to reach the works entrance. Go through the gap in the fencing behind the Woking Borough Council notice – which refers to Mill Moor Common – to reach a main road.

Turn right to reach a roundabout; this is Old Woking and a pub and the church lie ahead. The walk continues along Broadmead Road, to the right, going over a bridge. After about 50 yards, turn left through a gate and keep to the left of a concrete structure to reach the riverbank. Follow the bank, crossing some fencing when parallel to a distant brick building. Now head across marshy ground, passing one of the pylons and going under the overhead lines, to reach a causeway leading to Papercourt Lock with its cottage. There is usually plenty of activity here, and it is a delightful spot to sit and relax, watching the boats come and go along the canal, and rising and falling in the lock.

When you are ready to continue with the walk, follow the towpath past the cottage, staying with it all the way back to Cartbridge.

POINTS OF INTEREST:
If you would like to extend your walk, continue on to Send church (see Walk 1).

REFRESHMENTS:
The White Hart, Old Woking.
The New Inn, Cartbridge, at the start of the walk.

Walk 18 HEADLEY HEATH $3\frac{1}{2}$m ($5\frac{1}{2}$km)

Maps: OS Sheets Landranger 187; Pathfinder 1207 and 1206.

An exploration of part of Headley Heath, continuing steeply up to Mickleham Downs.

Start: At 205548, the Cock Inn, Headley.

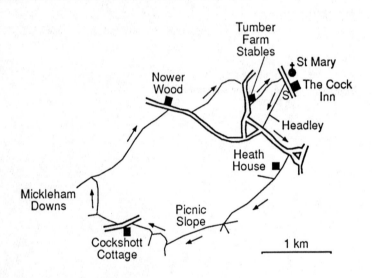

The Cock Inn is located beside St Mary's church, whose spire is a local landmark. Opposite the inn's car park, take the surfaced path by the bus stop. This brings you to a road by 'Ash House'. Turn left up the road, and continue around the double bend. *Great care should be taken, since there is no pavement.*

Opposite 'The Mint House', fork right to join a drive passing 'Heath House'. In the dip, by 'Garden Cottage', go up ahead, leaving the drive, which bears right. Follow this wide sand and stone track across Headley Heath.

At a six-way crossing with a marker post at its hub, take the broadest track ahead. This track soon rises to the top of a ridge, where there is an inscribed plank seat. Go down on a wide, stony track following a plain blue arrowhead, and passing a pleasant grassy slope on the right, an ideal place for a picnic.

At the bottom, continue ahead, but just around the bend, turn right, climbing up the wooded bank to reach a brick wall and a National Trust sign. Turn right and make your way down to a road, reaching it by the newly-renovated 'Cockshott Cottage'.

Avoid the very steep ascent immediately ahead: take the path going left above the parking area, through the narrow wooden barrier. At the end of a level, avenue-like section, bear right for the uphill slog to reach Mickleham Downs. This is a grand strip of upland meadow, which extends for over $^1/_2$ mile (800 metres) with a view forward to the spire of Ranmore Common church. An optional walk, adding 1 mile ($1^1/_2$km) to the walk length, to the end of the Downs and back is thoroughly recommended.

Turn right on to a track to reach a road almost opposite the entrance to **Nower Wood Educational Nature Reserve**. Go right for 200 yards, then turn left along another track. Beyond the cottage, continue to reach a road and go down to the bottom of the hill. Just past Tumber Farm Stables, go left through a kissing gate, and ascend back to the start of the walk.

POINTS OF INTEREST:
Nower Wood Educational Nature Reserve – This is an area of mixed woodland, covering 81 acres, which was purchased in 1971 by the Surrey Naturalists' Trust. It is now run by the Surrey Wildlife Trust, a registered charity, but is not generally open to the public. However, there are regular monthly open days (except during the winter) when all are welcome to visit and learn about the local nature. Specific seasonal topics are featured during these open days.

Information can be obtained from the Trust's Pirbright headquarters on 0483 488055, or from the Education Officer on 0372 379509.

REFRESHMENTS:
The Cock Inn, Headley.

Walk 19   PEASLAKE TO PITCH HILL $3\frac{1}{2}$m ($5\frac{1}{2}$km)

Maps: OS Sheets Landranger 187; Pathfinder 1226.

'He marched them up to the top of the hill, and he marched them down again'.

Start: At 086447, Peaslake village stores.

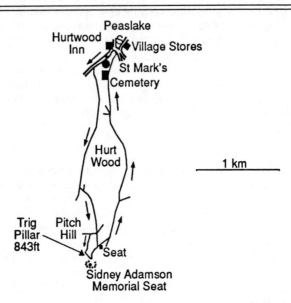

This walk takes you to the top of **Pitch Hill** with its magnificent views, by means of shady, sometimes narrow, paths and, in contrast, returns on a wide sandy track, fringed with heather, which provides vistas of the North Downs.

Start out along Walking Bottom, going past the Hurtwood Inn. Just beyond the last house, bear left off the road and pass through Hurtwood Control car park 2 and the pole barrier at is far end.

Stay on the main track, gaining height easily, for just under a mile (about $1\frac{1}{2}$kms). There are several crossing tracks on the way: ignore these, but look out for a fork, where the paths divide by the low trunk of a felled tree. Bear left here and join a track coming in from the left after a few yards.

When you emerge from the omnipresent woodland, turn right, and after 100

40

yards, turn left. Continue, to reach an oblique T-junction, where the triangulation pillar marking the highest point of Pitch Hill, at 843 feet (257 metres), is just up to the right.

There are different viewpoints to discover here, but perhaps you will agree that the best is on the spur where a seat in memory of Mr Sidney Adamson has been placed, since it offers a view through 225 degrees.

Take the path behind this spur, going northward, directly away from the view, and veer right to go past another vantage point where there is a metal seat. Turn down right at a marker post, following a blue GW (Greensand Way) arrowhead, then go left on to a wide sandy bridleway. Keep ahead on this bridleway from now on.

In just under a mile (about $1^1/_2$kms), a three way junction is reached: ignore the 90 and 45 degree left paths. Further on, you will reach the cemetery: follow the pathway from the lych gate down to St Mark's church from where it is only a short step back to the start of the walk.

POINTS OF INTEREST:
Pitch Hill – The hill is the most westerly of the three summits in this range. Leith Hill is the highest at 965 feet (294 metres), while in between, both in terms of height and location, is Holmbury Hill, 857 feet (261 metres).

REFRESHMENTS:
The Hurtwood Inn, Peaslake.

Walk 20 NEWLANDS CORNER AND THE SILENT POOL 3½m (5½km)

Maps: OS Sheets Landranger 186 and 187; Pathfinder 1226.

A rectangular walk, with quite a climb at the end.

Start: At 044493, Newlands Corner car park.

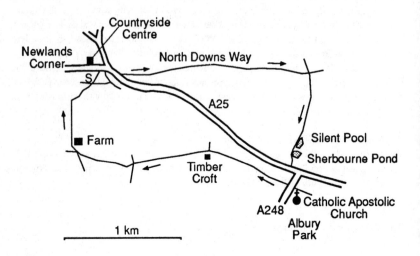

From the Countryside Centre, make for the grass below the vehicle exit and cross the A25 to join the North Downs Way. This stretch of the Way (see Note to Walk 28) offers level, easy walking suitable for everybody, but unfortunately, views are hard to come by due to tree growth.

The descent to **The Silent Pool** begins at marker post Number 5, situated at a crossing before the North Downs Way enters a dark wood. Turn right, and, a short way down at an obvious turn off to the left, take a few steps to get the best view: beyond the hillside, the **church** in Shere can just be discerned half-left.

Continue to post Number 6, half-way down the side of a field, then turn left to descend steps to reach The Silent Pool. A path goes all the way around: at the far end, continue walking to reach the main road (the A25) beyond Sherbourne Farm.

Cross the dual carriageway with care to reach the A248 and head towards the church ahead, using the pavement behind the hedge. At the crossing before the church itself, which is situated in private grounds, turn right across the road, and return towards **Newlands Corner** generally parallel with the A25, but at an ear-friendly distance.

At the next group of cottages beyond 'Timber Croft', go over the lane and climb the steep bank opposite. Continue, to reach a T-junction at the edge of woodland. Turn right to reach a farmhouse, and ascend the hillside to reach the start of the walk along a path running up the middle of the field.

POINTS OF INTEREST:

The Silent Pool – In contrast to the hustle and bustle at Newlands Corner, the Silent Pool is a small pond of very clear water encircled by woodland. There is a legend that a peasant girl used to bathe in the pool, but drowned in the deeper water when a wicked king chased her. The pool lies above another pond beside Sherbourne Farm, where there is a Farm Animal Centre. Visitors, without their dogs, are welcome at the Centre between 10 am and 6 pm, Tuesday–Sunday.

Church – The Catholic Apostolic, or Irvingite, Church situated beside the A248 in the privately-owned grounds of Albury Park, was built in 1840. The owner of Albury Park at that time, Henry Drummond, had it built – followed, two years, later by another church in Albury village – as his religious beliefs had moved away from those of the Church of England towards the communion founded by Edward Irving.

The parish church until then had been the one located beside Drummond's Mansion. This church, which dates from Saxon times, is not on the route of the walk. This church had fallen into a state of disrepair, so Drummond proposed a new parish church to be sited in the village for the convenience of the local community and an 'Apostles' Chapel' to be used by those sharing his beliefs.

Regular services are today held in the 'new' parish church, but the last service in the Apostles' Chapel was held in 1950, and in the Saxon church in 1841, though it is still the venue for occasional worship, particularly on the Sunday nearest to Midsummer's Day. The old church has undergone considerable restoration and repair and merits a separate visit.

Newlands Corner – This spot, on the A25 and at a height of 567 feet (173 metres), is one of Surrey's most accessible viewpoints. Recently, it has seen the addition of a Visitor Information Centre and snack-bar.

REFRESHMENTS:

The Newlands Corner café at the start of the walk.

Walk 21   AROUND CHALDON   3³/₄m (6km)

Maps: OS Sheets Landranger 187; Pathfinder 1207.
A level walk through farmland.
Start: At 308557, Chaldon church.

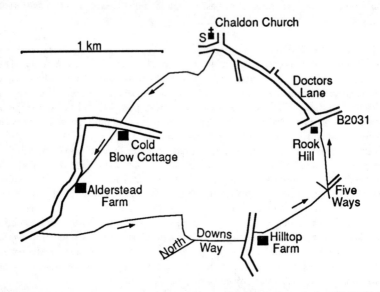

This is one of two walks starting and finishing at **Chaldon church**. See Walk 67 for the other.

From the churchyard entrance walk up to reach a stile just before the approach to Court Farm. Go over the stile and cross three fields to enter a wood. Bear left along an old concrete roadway to reach a road by the quaintly named Cold Blow Cottage. Turn right along the road for a short distance, entering a field on the left just before the Alderstead Heath name-board. Go diagonally across the field to rejoin the road at Alderstead Farm. Turn left along the road, passing the water compound and bearing right downhill.

Opposite 'Windfield', turn left down steps and follow the path out into open country. From here there is an interesting view down to the M23 and its junction with the M25, Surrey's very own 'Spaghetti Junction'.

Follow the path across several fields to reach a path junction just up from a house at Tollsworth Manor Farm. At the junction turn right along a track to join the North Downs Way. Follow the Way to reach a road opposite Hilltop Farm.

Turn left along Hilltop Lane for 75 yards, then go right beside a house named 'Pilgrims Lodge'. Now cross a succession of stiles and fields to reach Five Ways Crossing, which is marked with a prominent finger post. Follow the path signed for Rook Lane.

Cross the Lane (the B2031) to reach Doctors Lane and follow it downhill. At the bottom, take a right turn that will soon bring you back to Chaldon church.

POINTS OF INTEREST:
Chaldon church – The church contains the earliest-known English wall painting, dating from the twelfth century. It is believed to have been the work of a travelling monk and depicts 'The Ladder of Salvation of the Human Soul'. The square bowl of the font was carved by hand out of a single block of locally quarried Merstham stone.

Walk 22   DORMANS PARK $3\frac{3}{4}$m (6km)

Maps: OS Sheets Landranger 187; Pathfinder 1227.
A level walk taking in an estate of elegant housing.
Start: At 397415, Dormans railway station.

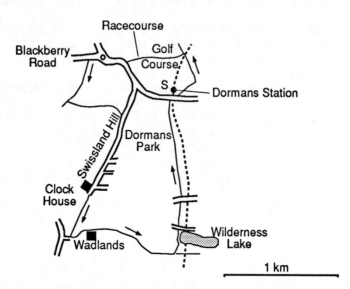

From the railway station take the surfaced path running beside the station house. When a crossing at the entrance to 'Nobles' is reached, turn left, going past a memorial seat dated 1992. Cross the railway bridge and turn left immediately, crossing a golf course and part of **Lingfield Park racecourse** to reach a road. Turn right and follow the road to a junction. There, take the road signed for Felcourt (Blackberry Road).

After about 50 yards turn left, taking a driveway around a new brick-built stable block. Follow the drive until it reaches a barn, then continue ahead, going up the grassland to reach the entrance to some woodland close to a large garden. Turn left down the line of conifers. Cross a stream and take a rising, shady path to reach a road. Turn right to enter Dormans Park.

Follow the road through the Park, ignoring all turnings to the left to reach **The Clock House**. Beyond the house the road narrows to a path; stay with the path, following it to where it ends, just before Felcourt Road. Turn left and walk past the second house (Wadlands), then turn right along a cindered path. Stay on this path to a point about 75 yards short of an arched railway bridge. There, turn left and walk along the edge of The Wilderness Lake. The view in this section of the walk includes not only the Lake, but the impressive Cooks Pond Viaduct. Continue along the path after it has left the lake, following the railway all the way back to Dormans station.

POINTS OF INTEREST:

Lingfield Park racecourse – The racecourse (Tel: 0342 834800) was established in 1890 and now holds race days every month with Turf, National Hunt and all weather racing on the 'Equitrack' surface.

The Clock House – The house was built at the end of the last century. Originally, one could drive a carriage through the archway into the stable yard, but this has now been filled in!

Walk 23   **FETCHAM DOWNS**   3³/₄m (6km)

Maps: OS Sheets Landranger 187; Pathfinder 1206.

A field and woodland walk, with a fine view at halfway.

Start: At 152549, the car park at the top of Leatherhead by-pass.

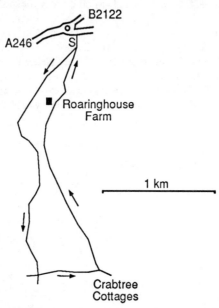

Turn off the drive to Bocketts Farm immediately past the top car park, walking along the track that is heading for the sawmill. Just after going around a bend, take the right branch at a fork, going under a canopy of trees. When a path crossing is reached, go ahead, and then pass under overhead lines. At the end of the field with the transmission tower (or pylon), bear left into a copse, and then take the track that follows the field edge.

At the fork almost at the bottom, take the right branch, going up the side of a field with Bookham Wood on your right. At the top, close to another transmission tower, walk into woodland and climb up a somewhat churned and narrow path. This path levels out, and then starts to descend. As it does, the spire of Ranmore church comes into view.

48

When a path crossing close to a stile is reached, the stile leading to a farm, do not cross; instead, go left and follow a path along the top of the slope to reach Crabtree Cottages, from where there is a fine view.

Now turn left along the track signposted to Bookham, and follow it downhill to reach a fork in the valley. Bear right and walk to the quaintly named Roaringhouse Farm. Continue ahead to reach the next path junction. Now turn up left, taking the path signposted for Fetcham, and follow the path back to the car park.

POINTS OF INTEREST:

View – The view south from Crabtree Cottages extends from Boxhill on the left across the Mole Gap, in which Dorking lies, to the continuation of the North Downs, where the spire of the church on Ranmore Common is prominent.

Walk 24   OUTWOOD   3³/₄m (6km)

Maps: OS Sheets Landranger 187; Pathfinder 1227.
A level walk, maybe for a Summer Sunday, when the mill is open.
Start: At 327456, the Outwood village sign, by the windmill.

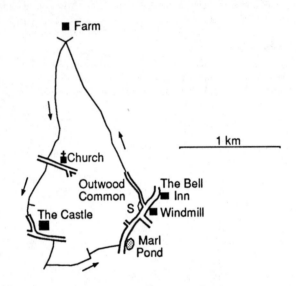

Walk along the green in the direction of Bletchingley and Godstone for 50 yards and turn left to pass by the cottages. At the fork, keep ahead to reach the aptly named Path End Cottage. Follow the path beyond through a belt of trees and over the crown of a hill. Maintain the same direction through a succession of fields to reach a path crossing in front of a farm. Turn sharp left, heading for the gate beyond the bridge with tubular railings.

     A gentle ascent now brings you to the end of the fields. Horses hooves may have made the approach into the wood rather muddy, but the brick and stone track beyond leads more comfortably to a path junction under overhead lines. Turn right and follow the path to reach a road. The walk continues along the footpath reached by crossing the road, but do turn left for 200 yards to see the Parish Church of St John the Baptist.

     The footpath across the road skirts fields to join a residential road, Bellwether

Lane. Go up the lane to a T-junction. Turn left along the road, passing The Castle. About 100 yards beyond The Castle, go right up a grassy path to reach a field from where there is a good view towards Gatwick Airport. Now descend, going towards the overhead lines, but turning left before them to go over two planks and a stile. Go up the side of a field and jink right beyond the tennis court. Maintain the same direction to reach a track. Turn up left and 50 yards past the stile and metal gates, go right along the top side of ground newly planted with protected saplings. Now go along the drive of Marl Pond Cottage to reach a road. Turn left to return to **the windmill.**

POINTS OF INTEREST:
The windmill – The windmill at Outwood is England's oldest working windmill, and dates from 1665. It is open on Sundays between 2 pm and 6 pm, from Easter until October.

REFRESHMENTS:
The Bell Inn, just beyond the green at Outwood.
The Castle Inn, Millers Lane, Wasp Green.

Walk 25   THE WEY NAVIGATION: WEYBRIDGE TO NEW HAW

3³/₄m (6km)

Maps: OS Sheets Landranger 187; Pathfinder 1190.
An easy stroll along a lower stretch of the canal.
Start: At 068647, Town Lock, Addlestone Road, Weybridge.

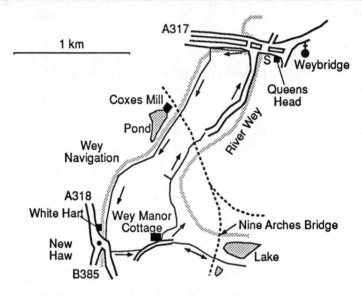

The two walks from Weybridge both commence at Town Lock, which is a short distance down Bridge Road from its junction at the end of Church Street (see Walk 88 for the other).

Set off along the towpath with the Navigation on your left. After ¹/₄ mile you come to Black Boy bridge: go over it and continue along the towpath. Pass under the low railway bridge to reach Coxes Lock and Coxes Mill.

A further ³/₄ mile stroll brings you to the road at New Haw. Follow the road to the left, around the bend, and take the footpath just before Wey Manor Fields. Turn left at the T-junction and keep ahead to reach Wey Manor Cottage. You may wish to walk forward to the railway embankment to have a look at Nine Arches bridge over to the left, and also to see the ponds just down the other side; if you do, return to the cottage.

Follow the track along the side of the cottage and then between cornfields, to reach a fork immediately beneath power lines. Bear right to reach the railway embankment, and go left on the other side, skirting the Riverside Park homes. Follow the drive between the brick pillars, and later beside the River Wey, to return to the start, where the river and Navigation unite.

POINTS OF INTEREST:

Coxes Lock – The lock is one of twelve on the Wey Navigation, which runs for $15^1/_2$ miles from Guildford to the Thames. Completed in 1653, the Navigation comprises some of the natural river course of the Wey, and nine miles of man-made canal. In 1764, a $4^1/_2$ mile extension to Godalming, with four more locks, was completed. The whole length of the combined Wey and Godalming Navigations is now owned by the National Trust.

Coxes Mill – The mill was originally built in the 1780s for the iron industry. In this century however, it was used as a flour mill. It was closed in 1983 and has now been converted into flats.

REFRESHMENTS:

The White Hart, New Haw (just across the bridge).
The Queens Head, Weybridge.

Walk 26   WAGGONERS WELLS $3\frac{3}{4}$m (6km)

Maps: OS Sheets Landranger 186; Pathfinder 1245.

A cross-border stroll into Hampshire passing through delightful woodland to see three picturesque ponds.

Start: At 874353, Grayshott War Memorial.

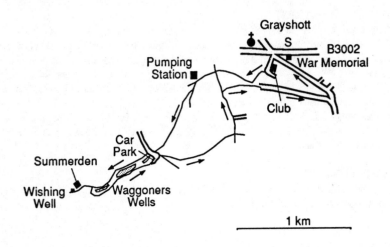

From the War Memorial, walk down Hill Road, passing the social club, then turn right into Stoney Bottom. At the foot of the slope, beyond the last bungalow, go right along a track. After $\frac{1}{4}$ mile (400 metres) fork left at a pumping-station, turning right on to a path after a further 75 yards.

The charming woodland path is followed easily to reach a road leading into the car park. Turn right and cross the ford, then bear left to walk beside the ponds known as **Waggoners Wells**. Follow the path beyond the third pond for 100 yards to reach a brick house, 'Summerden', with its Latin inscription *Dei Donum* (Gift of God). Bear left here to find the Wishing Well: may yours, fellow-walkers, come true!

Return to the top pond by means of the path on the other side, and go up a staircase into the car park to have a look at the map and to read the information board.

Leave the car park by the vehicle exit and turn right up a bridleway, going away from the ford. Fork left and ascend gently on a wide moss-bordered track to reach a crossing. Turn left up the steep slope to reach the end of a residential road. Keep ahead on a now level path.

Just as you start to descend, turn right, then fork left to drop down to the track which formed part of your outward route. Turn right, joining the surfaced part of Stoney Bottom and continuing to reach the junction at the top. Turn left to return to the War Memorial, Grayshott, with the spire of St Luke's church straight ahead.

POINTS OF INTEREST:

Waggoners Wells – The area around Waggoners Wells was acquired in 1919 as a memorial to Sir Robert Hunter, one of the founders of the National Trust. The origin of the three ponds is not known for certain, since they date back at least four centuries, when they were known, according to old maps, as Wakeners Wells. They were possibly intended as fish ponds. Today, fly-fishing for trout in the middle pond, and coarse-fishing for carp, perch, roach and tench in the upper and lower ponds, is allowed with the appropriate permits. The ponds form one of the sources of the River Wey.

REFRESHMENTS:
The Fox and Pelican, Grayshott.

Walk 27   **THE DEVIL'S PUNCH BOWL** $3^3/_4$m (6km)

Maps: OS Sheets Landranger 186; Pathfinder 1245.

A walk on National Trust land to discover what A3 travellers look over, yet overlook!

Start: At 891358, the Hillcrest Café, Hindhead, beside the A3.

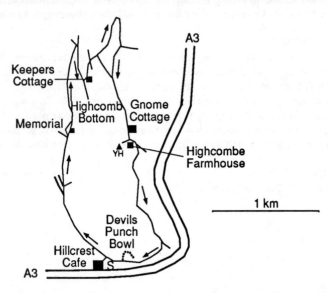

From the rear of the car park, walk past the notice board to reach the viewpoint. **The Devil's Punch Bowl** Nature Trail starts here: leaflets for it can be purchased in the café. However, this walk starts out along the upper left path, at the foot of the steps.

At the upright pole, keep ahead beside the paling fence to reach a seat placed at a spot where, through a clearing, there is a delightful view down to a 'Monopoly' house sitting on the grass slope. Shortly, the walk reaches the Highcombe sign, by the electricity sub-station: take the track which passes under a height barrier and follow the line of poles to reach a bench seat on the left. Just beyond, there is a three-way fork: take the right path to see the memorial, and then carry on to rejoin the track.

After a gradual descent, a right hairpin bend is reached. Go around this and proceed downhill. Near the bottom, by the field gate, turn left to pass above 'Keeper's

Cottage'. The track descends to a stream, which is crossed by a bridge. Climb up on the other side and turn left along a path barred to horses and cycles. Now do a clockwise loop to reach a track, and turn right to commence your return journey. A memorial seat to the Watkins brothers here allows you the chance to review your outward route through the woods opposite.

Continue along the track to reach 'Gnome Cottage' and a junction near to the Youth Hostel. Turn left, going around and beyond '**Highcombe Farmhouse**', seen as the 'Monopoly' house earlier, and bear right just after the bend, at the marker post and fire beaters.

Now follow the Nature Trail seen at the start, going in reverse around the open sides of the Punch Bowl and forking right at post Number 3 for the long-awaited ascent. At the top of the steps, turn right and enjoy an almost bird's eye view of the walk, before continuing to the car park.

POINTS OF INTEREST:

The Devil's Punch Bowl – The hollow is a natural basin formed by the erosive action of spring water over thousands of years.

Highcombe Farmhouse – The spelling of Highcomb/Highcombe varies: the obelisk, erected to record the bequest of Highcomb Copse by W A Robertson in memory of his two brothers killed in the First World War, omits the 'e', whereas the National Trust sign and the farmhouse display 'Highcombe'.

REFRESHMENTS:

The Hillcrest Café.

The Devil's Punch Bowl Hotel, on other side of A3.

Walk 28   SHERE AND GOMSHALL   3³/₄m (6km)

Maps: OS Sheets Landranger 187; Pathfinder 1226.

After a steady initial ascent, a comfortable walk along good tracks and paths.

Start: At 073478, The Square, Shere.

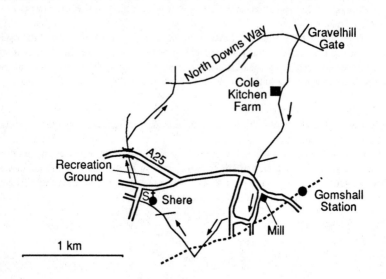

Cross the river and proceed along Middle Street. At the end, set in the wall, is the **Drinking Fountain**. Bear left into Upper Street for few yards, then turn right to reach the recreation ground. Follow the track beside this, passing under the A25 to reach a fork. Bear right, and climb steadily uphill all the way to the top, where there is a crossing. To your left is one of the concrete reservoirs, now empty, which, like the brick pill boxes, are relics of the Second World War.

Turn right on to the **North Downs Way** for almost a mile (about 1¹/₂kms) of level walking with firm ground underfoot, to reach Gravelhill Gate. Here, at a five-way junction, you find another reservoir and an inscribed seat. Turn right and commence a pleasant and shady descent to Cole Kitchen Farm, nestling in complete seclusion in the fold of the hills. The drive beyond joins a road which leads down into Gomshall.

Turn left along the main road to reach the Mill, and cross the bridge. Follow the road past the football and recreation grounds, and bear right by the railway arch to reach the High View junction. Continue along Gravelpits Lane, beside the gates of 'Monk's House' opposite. Go left at 'Gravel Pits Farmhouse', passing the tennis court, and cross the railway bridge. Now, make your way along the right side of the rounded field, then turn right through the barriers and back over the railway. The cross-field path points you towards Shere church, with a panoramic view of the North Downs. Follow the path back to the start point.

POINTS OF INTEREST:

The Drinking Fountain – The fountain at the top of Middle Street was constructed in 1886 for two local sisters called Spotteswood. The sisters wished to provide a free, non-alcoholic alternative to the beverages supplied by the White Horse. The well that was bored was 280 feet deep and water flowed until the 1970s, when activity in the neighbourhood by Thames Water brought about a lowering in the water table. The refurbished site of today results from local efforts in 1984.

The North Downs Way – This National Trail runs from Farnham to Dover, a distance of 141 miles. It largely runs along the top of the ridge, whereas the route taken by some pilgrims travelling between Winchester and the shrine of St Thomas à Becket in Canterbury Cathedral, would possibly have been along the foot of the Downs, where the inns were located. Today, waymarking is by means of the Countryside Commission's acorn logo. Underfoot, stretches of narrow and often muddy paths contrast with the firm surface enjoyed on this walk. The reason is that here the Trail follows a section of old drove road, used in bygone days to move sheep.

Gomshall Mill – The mill is an 11th century working water mill on the Tillingbourne. It now comprises a restaurant, tea-room and shops. The mill pond, which provided the power to drive the larger, 18 foot diameter wheel, has been converted into gardens overlooking the river.

REFRESHMENTS

The Compasses Inn, Gomshall.
Gomshall Mill – open 9.30 am to 5.30 pm. Tel: 0486 412433.
The White Horse, Shere.
The Prince of Wales, Shere.
Aster's Tea Shop, Shere.

Walk 29   THURSLEY   3³/₄m (6km)

Maps: OS sheets Landranger 186; Pathfinder 1245.

Charming village cottages, a sylvan glade and a viewpoint among the heather.

Start: At 902397, the centre of Thursley.

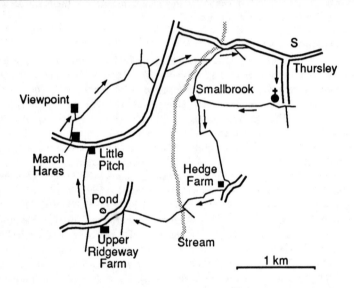

From the triangle of grass with its village sign depicting Thor, go along The Street to the church of St Michael and All Angels. Just up from the gates into the churchyard, take the footpath over the stone steps, and bear left around the wall of Hill Farm. At the end of some fields, drop down to the Smallbrook buildings. Turn left up a lane, keeping ahead where it turns into 'Haybarn'. In under 100 yards, turn left alongside a field, and, when you have crossed the stile, follow the yellow arrowhead up the right side of more fields to reach Hedge Farm.

Turn right at the road, but go only as far as the bend. Here, cross the stile on the right and skirt two fields before going down into a picturesque glade with a small stream flowing under a canopy of trees.

Cross the stream and climb a slope, passing Ridgeway Farm at the top. Walk

60

forward and down to reach a junction and continue ahead up Hyde Lane. About 100 yards after the pond at Upper Ridgeway Farm, turn right down a track which will bring you to 'Little Pitch'. There, turn left along a road.

Having passed the last bungalow, 'March Hares', turn right through a line of tree stumps. When more stumps are reached, turn right again on to a broad sandy track. Around the bend, a steep path goes up left, through encroaching bushes and heather, to reach a triangulation pillar: it is worth the climb for the fine view, and will only take a few minutes.

Return to the lower track and continue leftwards, ignoring a left fork under power lines. Descend gently under the pines, and then turn right to cross a fenced bridge. Take the narrow path between the roadway and 'Potters Pines' and follow it up to a road. Turn left for 100 yards, then go right on to a footpath that guides you to a rustic bridge. Go over a stile and continue to reach a charming miniature meadow. Cross a stream and another stile and turn left to reach a road. Walk uphill between cottages to reach a bend, and there take the path ahead. This path rejoins the road by the cricket pitch: turn right to return to the start of the walk.

POINTS OF INTEREST:

St Michael and All Angels – In the churchyard is the grave of an unidentified sailor who was murdered in 1786 by the three men subsequently hanged at Gibbet Hill. The story goes that the sailor, heading for Portsmouth, met up with three men and paid for their lodging and refreshment. He was last seen alive in Thursley and his naked body was discovered in The Devil's Punch Bowl. The men were caught further along the road, near Petersfield, trying to sell his clothes.

REFRESHMENTS:
The Three Horseshoes, Thursley.

Walk 30   BEARE GREEN   3³/₄m (6km)

Maps: OS Sheets Landranger 187; Pathfinder 1226.
A level walk between farms.
Start: At 176437, Beare Green pond, near Holmwood station.

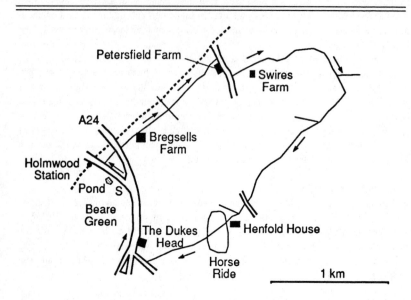

Walk up the road towards the station and turn right into Bregsells Drive. Pass under the A24 and continue through the farmyard into fields, keeping the railway to your left. A corrugated roof comes into view ahead: when this is 200 yards distant, go into the adjacent field, by way of the gate under the oak tree, and continue past the derelict buildings to reach a road.

Turn right past the entrance to Petersfield Farm, and at the next junction, turn left along the concrete drive to Swires Farm. Walk past the farm buildings and continue on a track which, in time, passes through a gate and then does a broad right turn into grassland. Keep the hedgerow on your immediate right all the way to the edge of the next field, which is likely to be under cultivation.

At the corner, turn right along a grass strip, still staying beside the hedgerow. At the end of the field, the grass continues ahead between woodland and bracken. Ignore a right fork by a marker post and carry on ahead to reach a plank bridge. Cross and go left on the other side to pass above a pond.

Once across the ford, keep ahead to skirt another pond. The path now enters woodland and you take a left fork uphill at a marker post to reach a road.

Cross to 'Henfold House' and, in front of the white gate to the house itself, turn right. Beyond the wooden barn, turn left to walk beside the garden pond. You will soon come to the horse riding circuit: cross this opposite a small seat and the gate leading from the lawn. Now go down the grass between the fences and cross the horse-ride again at the bottom.

Walk ahead now, going through three fields to reach a road. Turn right to reach the Duke's Head Inn on the A24, and then continue with care beside the busy road to reach a subway returning you to **Beare Green** pond.

POINTS OF INTEREST:
Beare Green – Beare is pronounced to rhyme with *bear* not *beer*.

REFRESHMENTS:
The Duke's Head, Beare Green.
Copperfield's Coffee Shop, in Beare Green Court.

Walk 31 COMPTON 3³/₄m (6km)

Maps: OS Sheets Landranger 186; Pathfinder 1225.

A walk around the village, near Guildford, noted for the Watts Gallery.

Start: At 956469, the Harrow Inn, Compton.

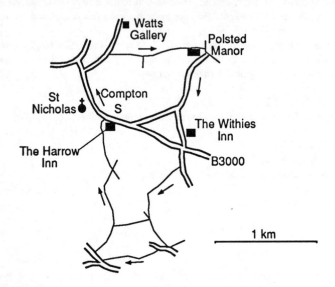

With the inn on your left, walk along the road in the direction of the A3, passing the church of St Nicholas. At Down Lane, turn right, following the sign to Watts Gallery, and walking past the cemetery. At Coneycroft Farm, continue along the road if you wish to visit the Watts Gallery. Return to the farm from the Gallery and take the footpath which runs alongside the wall, continuing beside the white-painted barn. Proceed to the far end of the concrete drive and turn right over a stile. Now go left over another stile a few paces later. Look out for yet another stile beneath an oak tree: go over on to a fenced path still going in the same direction. At the end of the path, by the garden, go down a few steps into a gully and turn right to reach a lane at the entrance to 'Little Polsted'. Continue along the lane passing Polsted Manor.

At the junction with a grass triangle, turn left to reach the Withies Inn, and then walk on to reach the New Pond Road crossing. Now go forward along The Avenue, but after 200 yards, turn right along a bridleway. Cross a diagonal footpath and then bear left after a drive. Walk between a mixed garden hedge and a hedgerow to join a track going around a field. Turn right at the field's first corner and exit it at the second, to be confronted by a fine sweep of grassland. Go uphill with this on your right to reach some trees, and climb the 60 steps in front.

Now keep ahead to walk along a dark and straight alleyway leading to a residential road. Here, turn right, then keep ahead at a bend to walk beside a playing field. At the junction with Hurtmore Road, turn right for 100 yards, then go right along a bridleway. Keep ahead at the gates to Broomfield Manor and take the path in front when you reach the 'Foxhanger' entrance.

At the T-junction at the edge of woodland, turn left through a kissing gate and continue to reach a track going over the crest. Half-way down the slope, cross a stile on the left, opposite a gate, and head diagonally towards the farm barns. Enter the next field via the stile over to the left of the gates, and proceed past the barns and down a field. Now go over a concrete stile to reach a path that leads directly to the Harrow Inn.

POINTS OF INTEREST:

The Watts Gallery – The prolific English artist, George Frederick Watts, 1817-1904, and his second wife, Mary, lived in Compton from 1891. He asked a friend to design a small gallery in the grounds of their house so that his studio collection could be preserved and displayed. The gallery was duly opened in 1904. Today it is open daily except Thursdays, from 2 pm until 4 pm, October to March, and until 6 pm, April to September; and between 11 am and 1 pm on Wednesdays and Saturdays. An adjacent teashop serves home-cooked lunches and teas between 10.30am and 5.30 pm every day.

REFRESHMENTS:

The Harrow Inn, Compton.
The Withies Inn, Compton.
There is a teashop at the Watts Gallery.

Walk 32   BOCKETTS FARM   4m (6¹/₂km)

Maps: OS Sheets Landranger 187; Pathfinder 1206.
A riverside stroll and a visit to the farm.
Start: At 167562, Leatherhead parish church.

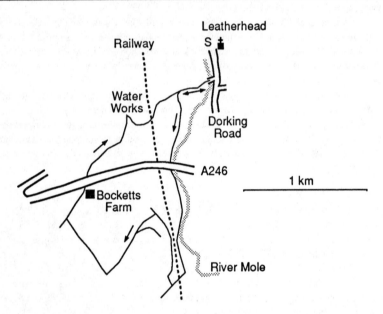

From Park Gardens in front of the parish church of St Mary and St Nicholas, go along the main road away from the town centre to reach Thorncroft Drive, to the right. Turn into it, soon crossing the River Mole. Walk past some buildings, beyond which a crossing is reached. Turn left here, following the sign to Norbury Park.

Go under the bridge which carries the by-pass towards Guildford, and continue through the picnic area. At the end of the picnic area continue ahead, going through a gate. Walk over the hill crest ahead and drop down to reach a gate. Go through and follow the track to reach a secluded brick cottage. Turn right over a stile and walk under a railway bridge. Continue along the path to reach a crossing. Here turn steeply up right to reach a gate and stile. Go through, or over, and then walk anti-clockwise around the sloping hillside to reach another stile at railway level. Go over and turn left, following the field edge for 175 yards to reach a gate on the left. Go through and follow the path beyond upwards.

After passing a group of yew trees, the path meets a track; continue past the bench seat and follow the bridleway around the bend at the barrier which guards the entrance to Updown Wood. Now descend to a T-junction and turn right towards **Bocketts Farm.**

At the farm, keep ahead on the concrete drive to reach the main road (the A246). Cross the road with great care and continue along the bridleway opposite as far as the junction by the water works. There turn right and cross the railway, heading for the church which is straight ahead. Soon you will reach a small vineyard beyond which the outward route is rejoined. Now follow the outward route back to the start.

POINTS OF INTEREST:
Bocketts Farm – This is a working family farm, but is also a Farm Park with old and new breeds of animals. There are outdoor paddocks and a large covered area where animals can be seen at close quarters. There are displays of agricultural bygones and craft demonstrations.

Opening hours are 10 am to 6 pm all year round, and there is an admission charge. For more information, telephone 0372 363764.

REFRESHMENTS:
There are tea rooms in the 18th century barn at Bocketts Farm. There are also places to suit all tastes and pockets in Leatherhead.

Walk 33   BOWLHEAD GREEN   4m (6½km)

Maps: OS sheets Landranger 186; Pathfinder 1245.

An easy walk passing some delightful cottages.

Start: At 917383, the crossroads in Bowlhead Green.

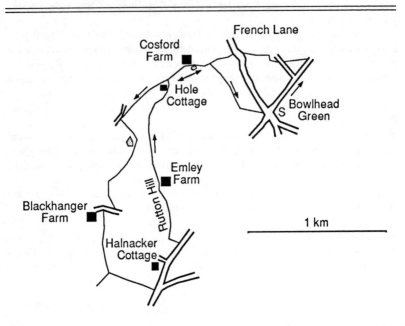

From the crossroads walk along the 'No Through Road'. At the fork, bear right to reach the gates of Lower House. Turn left, joining the Greensand Way. Climb up to cross a drive, continuing up the brick steps beyond and turning right around the field. Go over a stile, and bear left to reach a road. Cross and continue, dropping down quite steeply. After descending the rough-hewn steps walk beside a wall. The snug little pond on your left is home to a variety of water birds, and is overlooked by the delightful Cosford Farm.

At the bend in the drive, turn left and walk past Hole Cottage. At the crossing by the farm entrance, go left. Keep ahead at the fork, then drop down to reach a pond. Continue along the track to reach a U-bend. There, go right towards Blackhanger Farm. Soon after crossing a stream, go left over a stile and skirt the house and garden of the farm. Follow the overhead lines across the next field, exiting in the left-hand corner. Enter the woodland ahead beside one of the rusty iron **'P' gates**. Step delicately over a boggy patch, then cross a stream more easily on three planks.

The route ahead is obvious now, and is indicated by yellow arrowheads. When a road is reached turn left along it, keeping ahead (towards Emley) at the fork. Another charming house, Halnacker Cottage, is passed, beyond which you turn left along the drive to Halnacker Hill. Before the crest of the hill is reached, turn off right and climb up through trees to the top of **Rutton Hill**. Here a grand, all-round view rewards your effort.

Continue down the other side of the hill, heading towards the red tiles of Emley Farm, visible ahead. Turn left in front of the house and, below the parking area, go through a 'tunnel' of holly to reach a grass track. Walk along the track, veering left downhill. At a fork by another 'P' gate, go right, crossing the centre of the field. Follow the leaf-covered path beyond to emerge on to the hillside above Hole Cottage. Go downhill from here, and at the far left corner, turn right. Now retrace the outward route, passing Cosford Farm and the pond. However, at the finger post, leave the outward route, bearing right instead and staying outside the wood. This path climbs steadily uphill to regain the start.

POINTS OF INTEREST:
'P' Gates – The iron gates bearing a star, coronet and letter P, were erected by Lord Pirrie of Witley Park some seventy years ago, after he had been created a Viscount.
Rutton Hill – From the top of the hill you can look back to Gibbet Hill, the second highest in Surrey after Leith Hill.

REFRESHMENTS:
At Hole Cottage, Sandra Hanauer offers 'Hole Food', coffees, teas, and lunches for walkers. Closed on Mondays, but check otherwise on 0428 682881. Hole Cottage is passed on both the outward and return routes.

Walk 34   COLLEY HILL   4m (6½km)

Maps: OS Sheets Landranger 187; Pathfinder 1207.

*A walk along the top and foot of the North Downs. But be warned
–there is a stiff climb towards the end!*

Start: At 263523, the car park off Wray Lane at the top of Reigate
Hill.

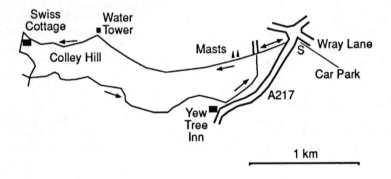

Leave the car parking area by ascending to reach and cross the white-painted footbridge.
Continue on the track beyond, the North Downs Way, to reach a crossing. Keep ahead
here, going past the two lofty masts.

Soon you come to a broad expanse of grassland, at the start of which there is a
12-pillared **shelter**. Continue along the track to reach a tower dated 1911 and inscribed
Sutton District Water Company. Here, bear left to walk on the grass in order to retain
the fine views to the south, but continue walking in the same direction. Further on the
North Downs Way is rejoined at a National Trust sign for Colley Hill.

Beyond, a white Coal Tax post (see Note to Walk 44) is passed; go left through
a barrier and at the roadway by Swiss Cottage, turn left. Go left again beyond the

gates, following the path between two black and white posts. Ahead now is a steep, but shady, descent on a good path. Continue to a path crossing, where the route leaves the North Downs Way; turn sharp left through the barrier and stay on the path which lies just above field level, ignoring all side tracks.

When a fork is reached it is wiser to use the right, stepped path, although both arms of the fork do join again later. Beyond a paddock, a residential road is reached close to another National Trust sign, this one for Pilgrims Way. Walk up the road to the hill crest and there bear half-left up the bridleway which runs up the left side of a brick wall. The bridleway leads to the main road (the A217). The Yew Tree Inn is about 75 yards down the road to the right.

It is easier now to use the main road, going left and uphill to return directly to the car park. However, it is far quieter and preferable to take the path that leads off at the end of the left pavement. This offers a stiff climb though, up to a path junction near the masts passed on the outward journey. From the masts reverse the outward route back to the start.

POINTS OF INTEREST:
Shelter – The shelter with its 12 pillars and dome, was presented to the Borough of Reigate by a Lt Col R W Inglis, and bears the date 1909. From its seats there is a fine view of the sweep of the North Downs.

REFRESHMENTS:
The Yew Tree Inn, on Reigate Hill road.

Walk 35   GODSTONE AND TANDRIDGE   4m (6¹/₂km)

Maps: OS Sheets Landranger 187; Pathfinder 1207.
A fairly level walk, taking in four ponds.
Start: At 350515, Godstone Green Pond.

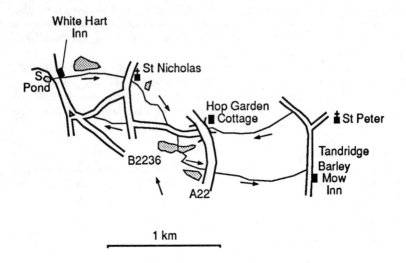

1 km

From the pond, cross the road and proceed along the right side of the White Hart Inn. Beyond the barn/village hall, you pass **Bay Pond**, and come to **St Nicholas' church**. Pass under the arch and to the right of the church itself. Leave the cemetery and descend to reach another pond, this one totally secluded this time. Beyond, the path bears right to approach an avenue of 15 conifers which leads to white ornamental gates; bear left uphill to reach an open field. There, turn right and walk down to a drive, continuing alongside a long brick building. When a bend is reached, turn right down to a lake. Cross the stile on the left and skirt Leigh Mill House to reach the garages. Take the gravelled bridleway past the tennis court and turn left between the hedges at the bottom.

Follow the paling fence above another pond to reach a gate leading to the busy main road (the A22). Cross the road with care and head straightforwardly across several fields to reach a road near Tandridge. Just to the right here is the Barley Mow Inn, but the route goes left and uphill through the village. At a road fork, with St Peter's church to the right, almost hidden from the road by the trees, bear left. Go down the road as far as the brick farm building with a bell over the archway. There, take the bridleway to the left and follow this to reach Hop Garden Cottage.

Go through the underpass under the A22 and keep ahead to pass the brick building seen on the outward route. At the end of the wall, follow the track round to the left and pass the entrance gates to Leigh Place. At the T-junction by Packhouse Cottage, go up the steps ahead to reach a field. Bear left to the crown of the field and then drop down, with St Nicholas' church visible over to the right, to reach a lane. Go left along the lane to reach a road. Turn right and follow the road back to Godstone Green.

POINTS OF INTEREST:

Bay Pond – The pond was dammed early in the 17th century to provide power for a local gunpowder mill. It is now a nature reserve.

St Nicholas' Church – The covered entrance to the church was erected in memory of G E G Hoare; members of this family served the parish between 1821 and 1930. It was restored in 1978 to celebrate the 50th anniversary of the ordination of K G Hoare.

REFRESHMENTS:

The White Hart Inn, Godstone.

The Bell Inn, Godstone.

Cream Teas are available at the Godstone Hotel.

The Barley Mow, Tandridge.

Walk 36 OAKS PARK AND LITTLE WOODCOTE 4m (6¹/₂km)

Maps: OS Sheets Landranger 187; Pathfinder 1191.

A well-signposted and easy walk along much of the 'Sutton Countryside Walk' route, opened in Spring 1993.

Start: At 275612, Oaks Park café, off Croydon Lane (the A2022).

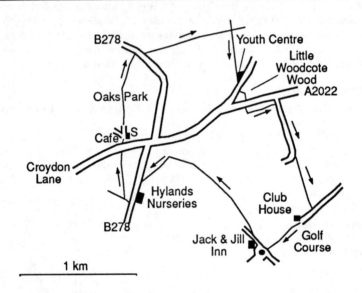

From the café, take the drive to the right-hand car park and proceed through the barrier, going downhill to reach a road. Cross to the right and continue up the concrete road into the smallholdings of Little Woodcote Estate.

At the crossing, turn right to reach another road by the Youth Centre and go across to skirt Little Woodcote Wood. At the next road, cross to Dell Cottage and turn left up the pathway under the trees to reach the drive to New Lodge Farm. Turn in here, and proceed along the dead-straight avenue of mixed trees to the bend. Go over the stile ahead.

Further stiles follow on this grassy path, which brings you to a road. Turn right, passing the golf club house. Follow the leafy bridleway beside the course to the beginning of the Clockhouse estate. There, turn right and 50 yards past the Jack and Jill public house, take the track to the right of the road.

Beyond the spiked gate, proceed along the left path to reach a track, from where there is a view to the skyscrapers of Canary Wharf, the City, and Central London.

Keep ahead beside the trees to pass a turning area. About 35 yards down the narrow path beyond this, turn left over a stile and walk across rough grassland. At the top, bear right to reach a road. Turn left, passing Philip's Farm to reach a 30 mph sign by Hylands Nurseries.

Turn right over a stile and go diagonally across the meadow beyond, and the next field to return to the entrance to **Oaks Park**.

POINTS OF INTEREST:
Oaks Park – The horserace, 'The Oaks', is named after the estate which occupied the site of today's park. The twelfth Earl of Derby organised races here. It was his name that was given to the more famous race, held during the same June meeting on Epsom Downs.

REFRESHMENTS:
The Oaks Park café, at start.
The Jack and Jill Inn, Grove Lane, Clockhouse Estate.

Walk 37   **CLANDON PARK**   4m (6½km)

Maps: OS Sheets Landranger 186; Pathfinder 1206.

A level walk, affording views of the gentler slopes of the North Downs.

Start: At 044512, the church of St Peter and St Paul, West Clandon.

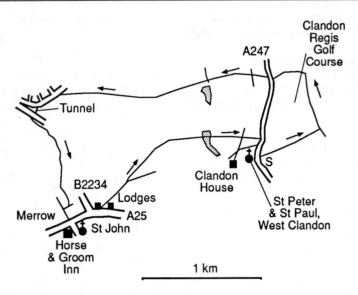

From the lych gate of the church, take the path between the cottages opposite to join a grassy lane. When you reach the far end of the field, turn left on the path at the other side of the drive. Stay on this path as it goes through the Clandon Regis golf course and around the back of the new buildings to return to the main road.

Continue ahead beside 'White Lodge' and then cross a track. Maintain the same direction at the end of the fields, crossing a stream by way of the ford or the footbridge. Please note that the lake up to the left here is private.

Further field-side walking, following the yellow arrowheads, now brings you to a wood-fringed residential road. Turn left past 'Henchley Dene' to reach a bend, then take the surfaced path on the left which leads under the main road through a tunnel.

Bear left and walk along a pathway through an estate of quality houses to reach some allotments, beyond which the church of St John the Evangelist, Merrow is visible. Turn left along Epsom Road to reach a roundabout, and enter the grounds of Clandon Park by going to the left of the left lodge.

Leave the drive by bearing left at a finger-post. The path leads across fields, re-crossing a track beyond the farm buildings of Temple Court. Enter woodland and cross a bridge over a pond. From the bridge you clearly see **Clandon House**, and glimpse the Ionic Temple, dating from 1838 and comprising six columns surmounted by a cupola.

Go over the drive leading to the House, and climb up to reach the main road (the A247). Turn right along the road to return to the church.

POINTS OF INTEREST:

Clandon House – The house, and part of Clandon Park, has been administered by the National Trust since 1956. The House (once described as a 'cube of red brick') was built in the early 1730s. The architect was the Venetian Giacomo Leoni, and there are distinct Italian influences. Inside, the Marble Hall is considered to be one of the country's best examples of an 18th century interior. There are also good collections of porcelain and furniture, and the museum of the Queen's Royal Surrey Regiment. The house is open daily from 1.30 pm to 5.30 pm, *except Thursdays and Fridays*, from 3 April to 31 October, and from 11 am on Bank Holiday Mondays.

The grounds were laid out by Capability Brown around 1770. Within the Park is Temple Court, the residence and working farm of the Earl of Onslow. The title was created in 1801, and today's Earl is the 7th holder, having succeeded his father in 1971.

REFRESHMENTS:
The Horse and Groom, Merrow.

Walk 38   CHURT AND WHITMOOR VALE   4m (6¹/₂km)

Maps: OS Sheets Landranger 186; Pathfinder 1245.
A charming woodland walk, crossing into Hampshire.
Start: At 855382, Churt crossroads.

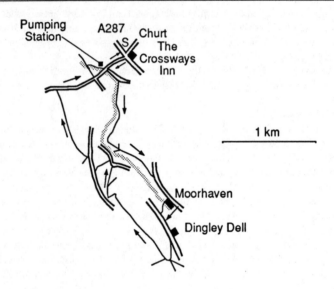

Take the Headley/Bordon road opposite the Crossways Inn and walk down to the Thames Water pumping station. Go left and walk uphill, passing 'The Old Mill'. At a fork, bear right along a bridleway to pass Barford Mill.

When the track curls right towards a house, keep ahead on a path above the lake. Continue past a cluster of houses nestling in a clearing to reach a road at the end of the drive. Now go forward for 200 yards and immediately before a house named Moorhaven, turn right and descend steeply to cross the stream that is the border between Surrey and Hampshire.

Climb up to a road and turn left. Just after passing a house called Dingley Dell, take the path branching half-right up the slope and follow it to the top. A barrier leading into grassland is now in front of you: turn right within the woodland and at the fork just beyond the overhead lines, bear right. Keep ahead at the wooden posts for a straight and gradual descent.

At the T-junction just beyond a broken pole-barrier, take the bridleway to the left to approach a road. However, before reaching it, turn sharp right in front of a gate and then bear left after 20 yards. Cross two stiles to reach the entrance to 'Walnut Well' and take the path on the other side of the drive, passing to the left of the garages. Follow the paling fence steeply uphill to reach a road by 'St Clares' and 'Cobwebs'.

Turn right for 100 yards, then, opposite the drive to 'Assisi', go left over a stile into woodland managed by Fountain Forestry Limited. Keep right at a fork and follow the path to join a drive which leads to a road by a gate marked 'Coombe Farm'. Turn right and walk to the junction with Hammer Lane. There, take the path on the left. Cross a **stream** and immediately turn right to return to the road at the pumping station. From there, retrace the outward route the short distance back to the start.

POINTS OF INTEREST:
Stream –The stream, which you cross, forms the county boundary between Surrey and Hampshire, and flows into Frensham Great Pond.

REFRESHMENTS:
The Crossways Inn, Churt.

Walks 39 & 40 DORMANSLAND AND DRY HILL 4¹/₄m (6³/₄km)
or 6m (9¹/₂km)

Maps: OS Sheets Landranger 187; Pathfinder 1228.
A hill walk with fine views over four counties.
Start: At 404422, Dormansland Post Office.

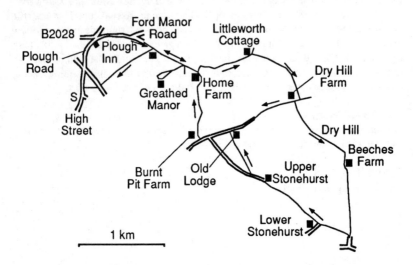

Walk down High Street and Plough Road to reach The Plough Inn. There, turn right
into Ford Manor Road. At the fork, bear right towards **Greathed Manor**. At the turning
to the house itself, go ahead on the rough track, soon forking to the left. At the next
fork, just before a house, turn left and then left again. About 100 yards after the bend,
the track goes left to reach another house; do not follow it, instead carry on up the
path into woodland.

Emerge from the wood through a gate into open country to reach Littleworth
Cottage at the crest of a hill. Descend for 50 yards to the first bend; turn right through
the metal gate, then fork left at the next. A steady ascent now brings you to the first of
a cluster of houses. Turn right at the T-junction to reach the end of the paddock.

For the shorter walk, keep ahead until you reach Old Lodge Farm, where you
rejoin the longer walk.

For the longer walk, turn left, climbing steadily to gain impressive views to both the front and behind. Above the East Surrey Water compound there is a trig pillar; this is the site of **Dry Hill Fort**, the ramparts still visible to the right. The obvious descent line now leads around Beeches Farm and down a lane past Woodlands House to within 100 yards of a road junction. At this point Kent is just a few yards away, beyond the stream to the left. The walk does not trespass; look out for the footpath sign on the right, taking the path across a field and through a wood, maintaining the same direction on a more neglected path to reach the drive of Lower Stonehurst Farm.

At the farm continue ahead, passing a bungalow and both wood and brick built stables. A gentle ascent through pasture will now bring you to Upper Stonehurst. Follow the drive into the dip, then turn off right through a field and wood to reach a path that climbs up to Old Lodge Farm on the top of a ridge. There, turn left on the road, rejoining the shorter walk.

Just before Burnt Pit Farm, turn right through the wooden gate, going past a barn. Continue downhill, bearing to the right to enter woodland. An easy descent now reaches the outward route close to Home Farm; reverse the route past the entrance to Greathed Manor, going as far as the stone pillars. Now turn left beyond the lodge and walk to the second road crossing. There, turn left to return to the start.

POINTS OF INTEREST:

Greathed Manor – The manor was built in the 1860s and, although a private residence, is open to the public between May and September on Wednesdays and Thursdays from 2 pm to 5 pm. Tel: 0342 832577.

Dry Hill Fort – The fort is believed to have been in use as a hilltop camp as long ago as the 1st or 2nd centuries BC.

REFRESHMENTS:

The Royal Oak, Dormansland.
The Plough Inn, Dormansland.

Walk 41 TILFORD AND FRENSHAM LITTLE POND 4¼m (6¾km)

Maps: OS Sheets Landranger 186; Pathfinder 1225.

A level walk through woods and by the River Wey.

Start: At 873435, Tilford village green.

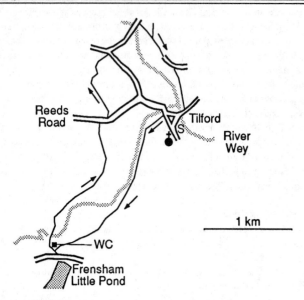

With your back to the Barley Mow Inn, turn right to reach the corner of the Green and cross to reach a short gravel track. Beyond the gate to the Malt House, veer left, then immediately go right, down a grassy path to a wooden gate. Continue ahead through woodland to meet the River Wey. When the path joins a wide track, turn right, and after a few yards take the left branch at a path fork. Just past the last house, go ahead, leaving the track which turns left into private land. When a low stile is reached, go over and turn right along a sandy bridleway.

After ¹/₂ mile, a brick-built public convenience is reached. The route continues from here by turning right, but first, do enjoy a leisurely stroll around the shores of Frensham Little Pond. One side is fringed with shady trees, whilst opposite are a number of small coves.

The path to the right goes past a cottage and then crosses the River Wey on a footbridge. Pass through a farmyard and keep right through a gate. Now follow a path that offers a pleasant walk through the forest to join a track leading out on to a road. Cross straight over the road to reach a path opposite and follow this to reach another road.

Cross and follow Sheephatch Lane opposite, following it to a bridge. Just over the bridge, take the path going up and right. Stay on this path until it meets a surfaced lane. Go forward to pass an impressive house on the left. At the end of the stone wall, turn off right down a footpath and follow it to reach a road. Go right along the road, crossing over the River Wey again to reach the start of the walk on **Tilford Green**.

POINTS OF INTEREST:
Tilford – The village is the point where the two branches of the River Wey join. One has started out in Hampshire, not far from Alton, while the source of the other is in the border area with West Sussex, south of Haslemere.

REFRESHMENTS:
The Barley Mow Inn, Tilford.

Walk 42 AROUND HASCOMBE AND HASCOMBE HILL   4¼m (6¾km)

Maps: OS Sheets Landranger 186; Pathfinder 1246 and 1245.

A couple of ascents are made worthwhile by secluded countryside and fine views.

Start: At 002394, the White Horse Inn, Hascombe.

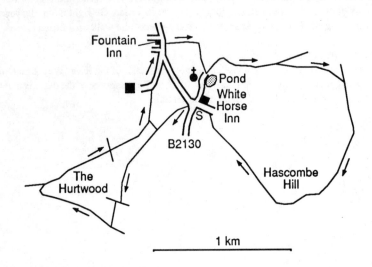

From the inn, cross the road and follow the finger post to the gate and grass beyond: you are now on the Greensand Way. Climb to the wood and fork right after a stile, and right again after a short, but stiff, climb.

When you reach the crest, another marker post with a blue GW arrowhead points right. Do not follow it: instead, keep ahead. At the offset crossing, looking at first like a T-junction, turn right, then left, and turn right at the following T-junction to emerge from woodland to an expanse of bracken.

When you reach a broad track after re-entering woodland, turn right along the straight horse-ride. Continue ahead at the wide crossing to reach a marker post at the top of a descent. Go down ahead following the cindered bridleway as it winds down to join a lane near the entrance to a house.

At the end of the lane, you reach **Hascombe** village by the fountain. Take the footpath opposite and cross the stream that ran refreshingly beside you along the lane. Head for the houses ahead: once you are past these you will catch sight of the spire of St Peter's church. However, before reaching the church or the pond close to it, turn left at the saw-mill, going up a bridleway. After some minutes' ascent, ignore a left fork leading to a pole carrying overhead lines, but do stop to look at the sweep of grass and woodland on both sides of the ridge.

A level but muddy section follows at the top of the further ascent: continue to join a path coming in sharply from the left. The view to the right is very pleasant as you progress, and glimpses through, and over, the trees to your left show that you have indeed climbed quite considerably. However, a little bit more climbing is still to come!

At the end of the field, you reach a crossing path which falls away on both sides. Continue half-right ahead, ascending quite steeply through mixed woodland to reach the upper slopes of Hascombe Hill. Here you can enjoy prolonged views as you progress along a level path fringed with bracken, foxgloves, and other wild flowers.

Curl clockwise around the hill with fine views all the while, including a glimpse of the top of St Peter's spire from a point just before a gradual descent through rhododendrons begins. At a fork lower down, go ahead on the upper, narrower path, then bear right down a gully. Cross the stile at the end and turn left down the lane to reach Hascombe and the White Horse.

POINTS OF INTEREST:
Hascombe – The fountain in the village was built in 1877 by Edward Rowcliffe, a local man, in remembrance of his brother Henry. A plaque commemorates the Queen's silver jubilee exactly one hundred years later.

REFRESHMENTS:
The White Horse Inn, Hascombe.

Walk 43 EFFINGHAM JUNCTION AND LITTLE BOOKHAM COMMON

$4^1/_4$m ($6^3/_4$km)

Maps: OS Sheets Landranger 187; Pathfinder 1206.
A level walk taking in fields, woodland and common land.
Start: At 102560, the Lord Howard Inn, Effingham Junction.

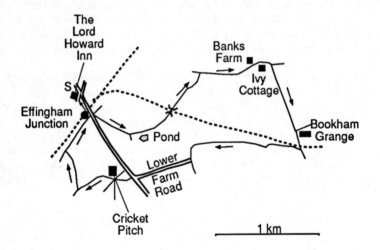

Walk along Howard Road opposite the inn and cross the railway bridge. By the bus shelter beyond the station car park, turn left along a drive, but after 25 yards, turn right on to a footpath.

Emerging from a wood, keep ahead over a farm track to pass a lawn-fringed pond. Beyond the fencing, walk along a strip of grassland, divided by a channel with bulrushes. Go through the low railway arch: you may find llamas grazing in the fields beyond!

Soon you will arrive at a track at the end of more woodland. Turn right to pass the National Trust sign for Bank's Common, and continue to the line of posts. Banks Farm is the brick house on the left. Carry on past Ivy Cottage, which has a helicopter pad in the garden. At the National Trust sign for Bookham Common, keep right on the track past the circular 'No Riding' notice.

When you reach a junction by the Bookham Grange Hotel, proceed right along Maddox Lane and cross the railway bridge. Immediately beyond, turn right along a footpath which tends to be rather overgrown. At the field at the bottom, bear left, crossing the channel on the five concrete posts. Now turn right across the stile, continuing to join a track in the next field and then heading for the thatched house, called Honeypots. Walk along the avenue and cross the main road at its end. Continue by going along the drive to 'Squirrels' and 'Tyrrells', then bearing right across the grass to reach the cricket pitch. Pass the pavilion and scoreboard, then cross the stile under the trees. Go straight ahead to reach a path at the edge of the wood and turn right to reach a line of bungalows. Turn right through the trees to reach the station car park from where it is a short step back to the **Lord Howard Inn** and the start.

POINTS OF INTEREST:

The Lord Howard Inn – The Lord referred to in the name of the inn at the start of the walk, is Charles, who lived between 1536 and 1624. He was a cousin of Queen Elizabeth the First and was Lord High Admiral and the commander-in-chief of the English fleet which defeated the Spanish Armada in 1588.

REFRESHMENTS:
The Lord Howard Inn, Effingham Junction.

Walk 44   WALTON HEATH   4¹/₄m (6³/₄km)

Maps: OS Sheets Landranger 187; Pathfinder 1207.

A level walk, returning beside the famous golf course.

Start: At 227553, Walton-on-the-Hill pond.

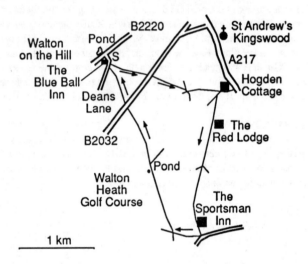

Walk along the path parallel with Deans Lane, to pass to the left of the sign for the Blue Ball Inn. Go over the surfaced path and fork slightly left. In 50 yards you will come to some trees: take the middle of the three paths ahead (the right-hand one is restricted by two upright posts).

Walk to the busy B2032, at the top of a dip with double white lines, and cross with care. Continue around the wooden pole barriers and head across the grass in the direction of the masts on the skyline, which are located at the top of Reigate Hill.

The spire of St Andrew's church, Kingswood, which has been prominent to your left, disappears behind a clump of trees as you approach the woodland and bear down a wide grass track to reach the bottom corner.

At this crossing, turn left along a 'dual carriageway' of path and horse-track to reach the end of a lane at 'Hogden Cottage'. Turn right at the **Coal Tax Post**, and take the left fork soon after. The path narrows and rises to a substantial house, The Red Lodge. At the bottom of its garden, go ahead to the far end of a field, and continue into the woodland. A shady path now winds through the trees to reach a bench seat. This has been placed facing a gap in the hedgerow, through which you can look across the grass and heather to woodland, with no visible sign of human hand, and only the incessant murmur of the M25 to interrupt your reverie.

After walking past two more benches, you will spy a white barrier, close to which is the Sportsman Inn. Go almost to the end of the road, then turn right along a bridleway. Just before the path crosses an arm of the golf course, turn right at another Coal Tax post. It is now a straight walk back, with the golf course always to your immediate left, and several more Posts, as well as a mini-pond to look out for.

Recross the B2032 by the entrance to 'Walton House', and take the footpath through the barriers. This leads back to the start of the walk, and the last Coal Tax Post, to be found next to the shop.

POINTS OF INTEREST:

Coal Tax Post – The white Coal Tax Posts, or Boundary Marks, are reminders that the Corporation of the City of London had the right, up until 1890, to levy a duty on coal brought into the City. This duty helped to pay for the rebuilding of several churches damaged in the Great Fire of 1666. After an Act of Parliament passed in 1861, the area for collection of duty was enlarged, and over 200 posts were erected. The ones seen on this walk bear this date and the name of the Regents Canal Ironworks. Other markings refer to the indexation of 'The London Coal and Wine Continuance Act, 1861', which was passed in the 24th/25th years of Queen Victoria's reign.

REFRESHMENTS:

The Sportsman, Mogador.
The Blue Ball Inn, Walton-on-the-Hill.

Walk 45   OCKLEY AND VANN LAKE $4\frac{1}{4}$m ($6\frac{3}{4}$km)

Maps: OS Sheets Landranger 187; Pathfinder 1226 and 1246.

A woodland walk with views to Leith Hill, and a visit to a nature reserve.

Start: At 148402, the Red Lion Inn, Ockley.

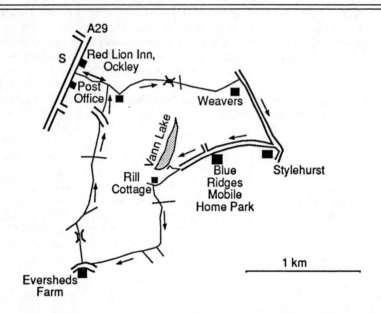

Between the inn and 'The Old Bakery and Post Office', take the footpath which ascends to a field. Keep to the right side of this as far as the crest, and then make for the gate to the left of a white house. Follow the fencing downhill to the bottom corner. Go through the gate, and follow the bridleway beyond to a bridge.

Climb the slope on the other side, ignoring a path off to the right. At the field corner at the top, take the path in front. This continues to a series of paving stones around a garden and then joins a road at the entrance to 'Weavers'.

Turn right along the road, walking as far as the letter box at 'Stylehurst'. There, turn right along a lane to reach the Blue Ridges Mobile Home Park. Keep ahead at the junction soon after, and a few yards past the entrance to 'Herons March', you will come to steps leading down, to the right, to **Vann Lake**. Having walked around part of the shore, and perhaps had a rest on the Maurice Ridgers memorial seat, return to the top of the steps and continue down the lane to reach 'Rill Cottage'. By the wooden shed lower down in the garden, turn left through a squeezer to discover a small pond. Climb the little bank on the right of this and then continue up a wider track.

Go straight over at a crossing, and, at a fork beyond the second of two slender white-topped posts, turn right, following a blue arrowhead. After 150 yards you will reach a T-junction at the edge of the wood: turn right here and, after another 150 yards, exit into a field. Now go ahead to join the track leading to Eversheds Farm.

Just before the Atcost barn, cross the stile on the right and aim for the left corner. Descend gradually in the woodland and cross a wooden bridge with tubular railings. Bear left up the slope beyond to reach a crossing. Turn right up the cart track, bearing left after 50 yards into woodland. Keep ahead to reach a field gate. Go through and ascend towards a line of houses. Exit through a gate in the right corner, and continue up a track. Cross a drive and follow the path to the top of a field. There, bear left to cross a stile after 20 yards. Half-way along the second field you will rejoin the outward route: now reverse the outward route back to the start.

POINTS OF INTEREST:

Vann Lake – The lake was originally constructed in the 18th century to provide water power. Now it is a nature reserve. An information board explains that the following creatures and plants are amongst those that have been, or may be found: 16 different species of dragonfly; mandarin duck; woodcock; kingfisher; sparrowhawk; butterflies such as purple emperor, silver-washed fritillary, white admiral; fungi; oak; hazel; alder.

REFRESHMENTS:

The Red Lion Inn, Ockley.

Walk 46 RIDDLESDOWN AND HAMSEY GREEN 4¹/₄m (6³/₄km)

Maps: OS Sheets Landranger 187; Pathfinder 1191 and 1207.

Riddlesdown is a popular area to exercise the dog, but you will see sheep and cattle as well.

Start: At 325605, Riddlesdown car park.

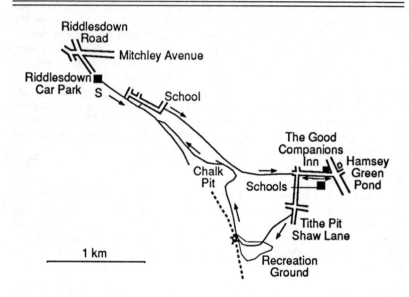

The car park is at top of Riddlesdown Road.

Leave the car park along the path and keep ahead at a finger-posted fork. By the last house, however, turn left through the stumps, go up to the road and turn right. At a bend, go left towards the High School, but turn right along a bridleway before the electricity sub-station.

Keep ahead at the end of the playing field and follow a level, and fairly straight path to meet a road. Go along this for 400 yards to reach Hamsey Green, where the Good Companions Inn will be found facing a small pond across the main road.

Return along Tithe Pit Shaw Lane to the bend, and then continue around to go past the schools entrances,. At the commencement of the grass verge on the right, cross a stile. Go down into a wood beyond the grass, and, after 20 yards, take the right-hand path which descends quite steeply to reach a large recreation area with tennis courts.

Find the fork in the surfaced path by the children's enclosed play areas, and walk away from these and the pavilion to reach a corner. Do not go through the arch here: instead, continue on the path through the trees, walking parallel with the railway line.

A steady ascent now brings you to fencing surrounding a deep, disused chalk pit. Go anti-clockwise around this to reach a picnic table and seat at the farther top corner. Now fork half-left in the direction of the metal tower on the next ridge. Go down the slope to reach a double pole barrier, passing through it and following a level path across grassland to reach a fenced grazing area. You will now merge with a main track coming up from the left. Proceed gently uphill back to the car park.

POINTS OF INTEREST:
Sheep have been introduced to Riddlesdown, since they are considered to be more ecologically-friendly than grass control by mowing. They keep the encroaching scrub at bay, and are less of a disturbance to insects such as butterflies, crickets and grasshoppers, and other flora and fauna. The breeds grazing on the slopes are Jacobs (usually horned) and Southdown. You may also see cattle, either the red Sussex breed or Dexters.

REFRESHMENTS:
The Good Companions Inn, Hamsey Green.

Walk 47   **RUNNYMEDE**   4^1/$_4$m (6^3/$_4$km)

Maps: OS Sheets Landranger 176; Pathfinder 1173 and 1174.

A riverside walk and visits to three memorials to great events of history.

Start: At 996718, Coopers Hill car park, Englefield Green.

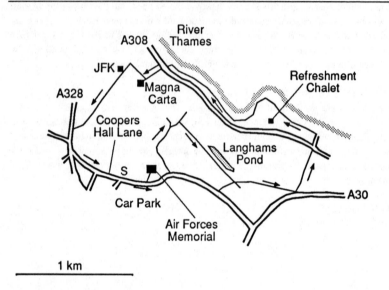

1 km

The **Air Forces Memorial** is only a short distance along the road from the car park where this walk commences. Having visited it, carry on around the left bend to a T-junction and turn left there, through the gate by the National Trust sign for Cooper's Hill Slopes. Flights of steps now take you down through woodland to reach a stile. Cross this stile, but ignore another to the immediate left, and go forward to the gate ahead. Do not go through: instead, turn right in front of it.

At the end of the line of trees on the left, you will reach Langham's Pond: continue ahead to its far end and then walk on to reach a crossing of paths. Turn left on to the one which has come down the hillside to cross a stile and a concrete bridge. Fork right beyond the bridge towards the line of houses facing the A30. Just before reaching the road, turn left along surfaced footpath number 12 to reach the A308, Windsor Road.

Go forward along Yard Mead to reach the riverbank and turn left. Now stay by the water's edge, with a possible diversion for refreshments at the cafeteria by the entrance to the Runnymede Pleasure Grounds, and cross the grassland contained within the bend in the river.

Having drawn level with the Air Forces Memorial, the pillars and lodges marking the limit of **Runnymede** come into view ahead, with the Magna Carta memorial half-left. Cross the road at the end of the fencing and visit the rotunda, then continue to the right to climb a cobbled path leading to the **JFK memorial**.

Continue on the path rising to the left behind the inscribed stone to join a drive that skirts the private grounds of Brunel University to meet a road. Turn left and follow the road to the crest, then go left again, into Coopers Hill Lane, to return to the start.

POINTS OF INTEREST:

Air Forces Memorial – This Memorial, on the top of Cooper's Hill, was constructed in 1953 to a design by Sir Edward Maufe, who also designed Guildford Cathedral. It commemorates more than 20,000 airmen, killed in the Second World War, who have no known grave. Their names are inscribed along the sides of the grass quadrangle. From the tower there is a fine view of the River Thames and beyond, towards the reservoirs and Heathrow airport.

Runnymede – This is the site where, in 1215, King John signed the Magna Carta. This 'Great Charter' established the basic principles of British justice and inspired the constitutions of the USA and other countries. The monument was erected by the American Bar Association in 1957 and takes the form of a rotunda with eight columns, covering a stone inscribed 'To commemorate Magna Carta symbol of freedom under law'.

JFK Memorial – A short distance from the Magna Carta memorial is another, sculpted by Alan Collins and erected in 1965, to John F Kennedy, the US President assassinated in November 1963, aged 46.

REFRESHMENTS:

There is a refreshment chalet/cafeteria by the vehicle entrance to the Runnymede Pleasure Grounds, and a tearoom a mile further on, just beyond the route described, in one of the green-shuttered lodges beside the two inscribed pillars which mark the boundary of Runnymede.

Walk 48   BROCKHAM AND BETCHWORTH   4¹/₂m (7¹/₄km)

Maps: OS Sheets Landranger 187; Pathfinder 1226 and 1227.
An easy walk near the River Mole.
Start: At 197496, Brockham Green.

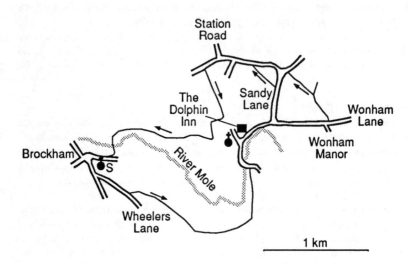

From **Brockham** village green, walk to the far side of the church. Turn left into Wheelers Lane and continue along it for three or four minutes. Now, opposite a green, there is a public footpath marked by a stone at ground level. The stone is not very obvious, but is just past the fourth part of 'Way House'. Turn left on this path and follow the edges of several fields before skirting a wood. At the end of the wood there is a stile. Go over this for a very pleasant view of the River Mole and the North Downs. Cross the field beyond the stile to reach a fenced thicket and keep the fence hard by on your left side. When a corner is reached, go over the first of two stiles, then cross a field to reach a road beside a bridge. Turn left and continue to Betchworth and the Dolphin Inn.

Turn right down Wonham Lane, using the footpath above the road. Pass the junction with Sandy Lane, to the left, and continue to the entrance to Wonham Manor.

Just beyond, on the left is a bridleway; follow this, climbing upwards. In under five minutes, you will pass through a gate; now go left immediately over a stile. Follow alongside a brick wall and, just after the house and in the dip, cross another stile. Follow the path for 150 yards to reach some steps; go down these to reach a road.

Turn left and 30 yards further on go left again at a bus stop. Pass the entrance to the Midland Group College and 75 yards further down the hill, turn right opposite the public footpath sign. Go to the top of the grassy ridge and cross a drive. In the next field make for the gate beside a greenhouse. Go through and follow a path. At the end of the path, cross a drive and turn left in front of a garage to walk between fencing. When a road is reached turn left.

At the junction with The Street, veer right, and at Station Road keep left. Fifty yards after the telephone box, outside the Post Office, turn left down the bridleway which is heading towards Betchworth church. At the bottom of the bridleway, turn right and cross a three-bar iron gate, following the yellow waymarkers. Keep the cultivated field on your right, with, at first, a high hedge and then a line of impressive trees on your left. After passing a wartime shelter the path heads towards some houses. Pass the back gardens of these houses to reach a track. Go down left and cross the River Mole. The surfaced path ahead will now lead you back to Brockham.

POINTS OF INTEREST:
Brockham – The village green is the site of one of Surrey's most famous annual Guy Fawkes' night bonfires.

REFRESHMENTS:
The Dolphin Inn, Betchworth.
The Royal Oak, Brockham.
The Duke's Head, Brockham.

Walk 49   GRAYSWOOD AND GIBBET HILL   4¹/₂m (7¹/₄km)

Maps: OS Sheets Landranger 186; Pathfinder 1245.
A walk up the second highest hill in Surrey.
Start: At 917346, All Saints Parish Church, Grayswood.

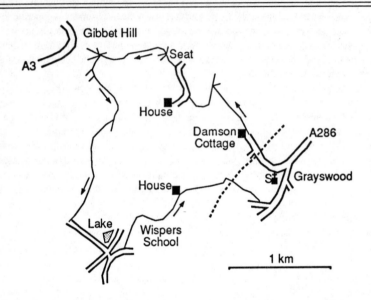

From the church, walk down the main road for 100 yards, then turn left along a public bridleway leading to Damson Cottage Farm. Pass through a railway arch after a few minutes, and then veer right beyond the gates. Keep on the drive to Damson Cottage itself, and walk across the gravel and around the house to enter woodland.

The path soon starts to ascend, firstly through pines, then across cleared ground, to reach a broad, sandy Forestry Commission track. Turn left up this and walk to a T-junction. Go right and walk to a bend. Here, go left, and bear left again 15 yards later for a short, but steep, climb. You are rewarded at the top with a seat.

Continue on the lower path behind the seat, passing a high metal gate. Keep ahead, with fine views to your right, to reach a junction. Turn right and walk for a couple of minutes to reach a 5-way junction. Go ahead through the pole barriers and after 30 yards bear right to reach the summit of **Gibbet Hill**, with its triangulation pillar and memorial cross bearing a Latin inscription.

Return to the barriers and go right, then left downhill. At the first fork, take the lower path which swings left. Keep on this path, bearing right beyond a marker post with three blue arrowheads, and, at the next fork soon afterwards, keep right. Ignore crossing tracks and at length emerge from the woodland. A short distance later, you will reach a road on the left: go down this to reach a charming lake at Inval House.

Cross the road beyond and climb to the crest of the hill. Double back left on the road to Wispers School, soon taking the bridleway on the left, which runs parallel to the road. At a fork, bear slightly right and ascend through a holly grove. Turn right at the top and descend gently. Bear left on meeting another path to reach a metal post with yellow arrowheads. Go ahead to reach a metal gate, followed soon after by a smaller gate, beyond which you turn right just before a house.

Cross the rounded field to its bottom left corner and continue down the gully. Walk past a small lake on the left, and descend to cross a rivulet on a rickety plank. Climb briefly to reach a crossing where a gate confronts you. Take the stile to its right and cross the small field beyond into the trees. Continue ahead to reach a gate and stile. Go over and climb up to cross railway lines. Follow the path beyond back to Grayswood, turning left at the main road to walk past the Wheatsheaf Inn.

POINTS OF INTEREST:
Gibbet Hill – at 892ft (272m), is the second highest in Surrey after Leith Hill. The name dates from 1786 when three men were hanged here for the murder of a sailor. The victim is buried in Thursley churchyard.

REFRESHMENTS:
The Wheatsheaf Inn, Grayswood.

Maps: OS Sheets Landranger 175; Pathfinder 1189.
A walk around the lake, with gardens as well.
Start: At 981688, the car park beside the Wheatsheaf Inn, on the
A30.

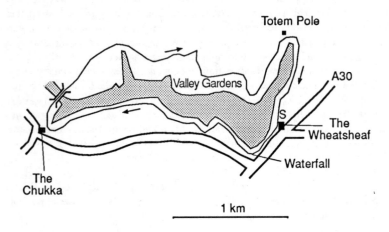

Virginia Water lies within Windsor Great Park. Part is in Surrey and the remainder in
Berkshire. It is an artificial lake, and was made in 1746 by damming and by the
diversion of several streams. There are numerous opportunities for individual
exploration, but this description is of a clockwise circuit of the lake.

From the car park make for the lakeside path and turn left. After 150 yards, take
the left fork to descend to the foot of a waterfall. Until now the route has been roughly
parallel to the A30; it now heads away from the road, following the lake shore towards
the remains brought from the Roman city of *Leptus Magna*, visible over to the left.
Originally the remains were located near Tripoli in Libya, but in 1818 they were
brought to England, and were erected here in 1827 at the direction of George IV.

Continuing along the shore, the Frost Farm Plantation is passed. It comprises mainly oak, beech, sweet chestnut and hornbeam, and has a thriving population of toadstools and insects.

Before reaching the graceful, five-arched bridge, the route passes the pink Blacknest Gate Lodge, built in 1834. Here a short detour can be made to The Chukka – go along Mill Lane to its junction with the A329 – the inn's name serving as a reminder of the polo-playing tradition within the Park.

The route continues along a straight drive, eventually curving around to cross another arm of the lake. Just beyond, take the path following the pointer to the Valley Gardens. This area provides a feast of colour, being planted with a great range of rhododendrons, camellias, magnolias and other trees, shrubs and herbaceous plants, which have been selected and planted with the aim of producing colour and interest throughout the year.

Nearing its end, the walk reaches the Totem Pole, which was presented to the Queen by the Canadian province of British Columbia to commemorate its centenary in 1958. From it there is about $\frac{1}{2}$ mile (800 metres) of walking back to the start.

POINTS OF INTEREST:
You may wish to extend the walk with a visit to the Savill Garden, also within Windsor Great Park and Surrey. It is acknowledged to be one of the finest woodland gardens in the world, and is open daily from 10 am. There is an admission charge. Tel: 0753 860222.

REFRESHMENTS:
The Wheatsheaf Inn, at the start of the walk.
The Chukka, near Blacknest Gate.

Walk 51   ALBURY AND BLACKHEATH   4$\frac{1}{2}$m (7$\frac{1}{4}$km)

Maps: OS Sheets Landranger 186; Pathfinder 1226.

An opportunity to discover the delightful area of Blackheath.

Start: At 048478, Albury Post Office, at the junction of The Street and Church Lane.

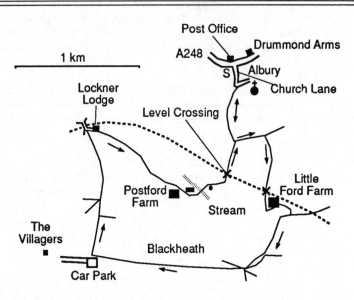

Walk up Church Lane, **Albury** and continue up Blackheath Lane. At the crest, take the sandy track to the left. After 300 yards go right at a fork, entering a field through a weighted gate. Follow the path beyond down to, and across, the railway, then use the sunken avenue between the trees to walk past a cottage, shutting the gates at both ends please.

Go past the barns and curve round to a T-junction. Turn right, taking a leafy bridleway up a small wooded valley. At a junction marked by a '237' post, walk ahead up the narrower path forking slightly right. Turn left when the path meets a wider track. The track leads into a triangular clearing, the hub of seven paths. Your exit is the fifth, counting clockwise, from your entry path as number one. After 75 yards, turn right at a marker post to follow the dead-straight bridleway, 302, all the way to a car park. Tracks and paths criss-cross the whole area of Blackheath, so tempting opportunities to wander off and explore abound, but, be warned, it is easy to lose your bearings!

At the car park, walk forward to reach a road. The Villagers Inn is 150 yards ahead, while the cricket pitch is to the left. Turn right however, to come to some roadside Seeboard equipment. Take the path opposite which runs alongside the private road. The path leads to Lingwood House. Continue ahead, to the right of the gates, and follow a path downhill to Lockner Lodge, just before the railway bridge. St Martha's Church juts into the sky ahead.

Turn across the drive and enter the field to the right of the house. A succession of undulations brings you to a house with prominent chimneys. Go down the track past the stables and cross the stream. Now walk up to another stable block, at the back of which cross a stile into the field on the left. Go diagonally up to the top right corner and cross the railway. Continue up the side of the next field to reach a stile just before the Dutch barn. Turn left on the lane, retracing your outward route to the start.

POINTS OF INTEREST:

Albury – Today the village occupies the site of an old hamlet called Weston Street. The original Albury clustered around the mansion a mile to the east, in Albury Park. Back in the 1780s, the then-owner, a Captain W C Finch, decided he wanted more privacy, and set about a series of actions which caused diversions to the road, and 'persuaded' some villagers to move out. A subsequent owner, Charles Wall, demolished the remaining cottages, and rehoused most of the residents in the homes he had built in today's Albury.

The Drummond Arms, in the village, derives its name from another owner of Albury Park, Henry Drummond, 1786-1860, who purchased the estate in 1819. He was a prominent banker, and Member of Parliament for West Surrey from 1847 until his death. He was a man of distinctive religious convictions, and built two churches, the one above the present village in 1842, and the other which can be seen from the road linking the park entrance with the A25. The last service here was in 1950. Drummond engaged the architect Augustus Pugin to give the mansion a thorough face-lift in the late 1840s. This included the ornate chimneys, more examples of which can be seen as you pass through the village.

REFRESHMENTS:
The Drummond Arms, Albury.
The Villagers Inn, Blackheath.

Walk 52 TADWORTH AND HEADLEY $4\frac{1}{2}$ m ($7\frac{1}{4}$ km)

Maps: OS Sheets Landranger 187; Pathfinder 1207.

A walk bisected by the M25, which does not however, mar the overall enjoyment.

Start: At 231562, Tadworth Station.

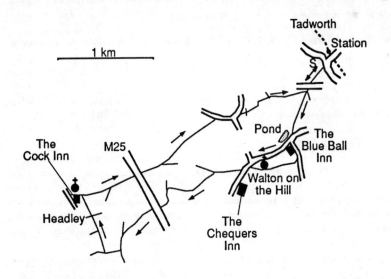

Walk up the path on the right of Barclays Bank to reach a road. Go right for a few yards, then turn left on to a bridleway opposite Spindlewoods. Take the wide track ahead, which initially runs parallel to a paved path to the left. Soon you will come to the pond at Walton-on-the-Hill, where pleasant moments can be spent on the waterside seats, watching the pond's birdlife.

Cross the road and go down Deans Lane, walking past the Blue Ball. The road bends right, and 50 yards later brings you to the Riddell Memorial Hall. Turn into Meadow Walk, and at its end, continue along a footpath to enter the churchyard. Beyond the lych gate, cross the green and proceed left along Chequers Lane. Just after the bend, turn right into Queens Close and continue ahead, going through posts. At the end of the paddock beyond the lawn of Walton Manor Farm, cross a stile on the left and walk ahead for 20 yards turning right beyond a fence. The M25, buzzing with traffic, is now in front of you.

Leave the field and follow the wire fencing round to the right, with the spire of **Headley** church straight ahead. Descend beyond a gate to reach a stile and go over on to a path going left. This path takes you under the motorway. Thankfully you soon lose the noise of the traffic as the path gently ascends on the fringe of woodland to reach a stile and gate. Just beyond is a track: turn left, heading for the farm buildings. About half-way to them, at the start of a small rise, go right over a stile to reach the end of the field. Turn right in between the next two stiles to walk to the church, close to which is the Cock Inn.

At the lych gate, turn right and descend, with a brief view of the grandstand on Epsom Downs to the left, to enter woodland. Continue to a track, and turn left beyond the stile to pass under the motorway again. Continue downhill, going under the power lines. At a wooden fence, turn left and skirt a paddock. Now climb to reach a road. Turn right and at the junction beyond the Hurst Road nameboard, bear left. After a few yards, turn right along a footpath beside 'Pilgrims Corner'. At the end, pass the barrier by a Coal Tax Post and fork left. Keep bearing left to rejoin the outward route just before Spindlewoods, returning to the station along the same alley followed on the outward journey.

POINTS OF INTEREST:
Headley – The village name derives from heather and lea, the latter meaning a pasture. The two churches on the route, St Peter the Apostle, in Walton-on-the-Hill, and St Mary the Virgin, in Headley, are worthy of inspection.

Coal Tax Post – The white Coal Tax Posts, or Boundary Marks, are reminders that the Corporation of the City of London had the right, up until 1890, to levy a duty on coal brought into the City. This duty helped to pay for the rebuilding of several churches damaged in the Great Fire of 1666. After an Act of Parliament passed in 1861, the area for collection of duty was enlarged, and over 200 posts were erected.

REFRESHMENTS:
The Blue Ball Inn, Walton-on-the-Hill.
The Chequers Inn, Walton-on-the-Hill.
The Cock Inn, beside Headley church.

Walk 53 BASINGSTOKE CANAL AND BROOKWOOD 4½m (7¼km)

Maps: OS Sheets Landranger 186; Pathfinder 1205.
A level, tranquil stroll.
Start: At 946559, Pirbright Green pond.

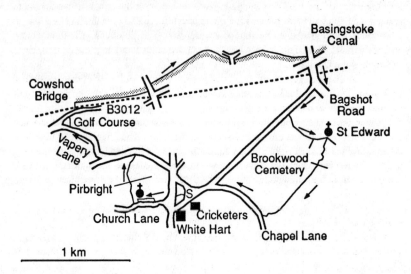

From the pond, walk across the green to the village sign by the red-brick Lord Pirbright's Hall and cross the road into Church Lane. Enter the churchyard at the first gate to see the grave of Sir Henry Morton Stanley and his wife. Return to the lane at the lych gate and turn right at the end of the wall to go along a footpath. When the path reaches a road, turn left for 250 yards, then go right along Vapery Lane. Near the end, just past the bungalow called Twin Oaks, bear right along a path skirting Goal Farm golf course to reach a road. Cross and walk through the tunnel under the railway, and, at Cowshot Bridge beyond, turn right along the towpath of the **Basingstoke Canal.**

Stay on the towpath for 1½ miles, crossing to the other bank at Pirbright Bridge – dated 1915 – to reach the busy Bagshot Road beside a petrol station. Turn right, go across at the traffic lights and walk under the railway bridge. Now fork right along Cemetery Pales for 400 yards to reach the entrance to **Brookwood Cemetery**. Turn in left and follow the drive to the St Edward Orthodox Church, dedicated to the martyr who died in 979 at Corfe in Dorset. Take the St David's avenue opposite and bear left at the fork by 'Colvmbarivm'. At the junction by the Bent memorial, turn right and go either way around the semi-circle. Follow the straight track ahead, going across a surfaced avenue by the St Alban shelter, to reach its far end. Go ahead on a narrow path into woodland, then bear half-right on a wide track which meets a lane beyond a pole barrier. Turn right to join a residential road, Chapel Lane. This leads to the main road and **Pirbright** Green where the walk started.

POINTS OF INTEREST:

Sir Henry Morton Stanley – Sir Henry (1841-1904) was born John Rowlands in Wales of unmarried parents. He ran away to sea, but was adopted by a New Orleans family called Stanley. He joined the New York Herald in 1867 and was later given the assignment to find the explorer, David Livingstone, who was travelling somewhere in Africa. They met at Ujiji in November 1871, Stanley uttering the now-famous line, 'Dr Livingstone, I presume?' He undertook many more African expeditions, before settling in Pirbright with his wife, Dorothy, whom he married in 1890.

The Basingstoke Canal – The canal was completed in 1794 and ran for 37 miles, linking Basingstoke with the River Wey Navigation near West Byfleet. The Greywell Tunnel, 1230 yards in length, partially collapsed in 1934 and now marks the terminus, some 5 miles short of Basingstoke itself. About one third of the canal lies in Surrey, yet the county has 28 of the 29 locks! Restoration work continues through the Surrey and Hampshire Canal Society.

Brookwood Cemetery – The cemetery was established in the 1850s because London's graveyards were full and, at that time, cremation was illegal. The London Necropolis Company purchased 2000 acres of land, of which 400 acres remain as today's cemetery, and ran 'coffin trains' from Waterloo to the present Brookwood station and then along a branch line, which no longer exists, to the graves. The mausoleums, pillars, and statues are a fascinating insight into how the Victorian age viewed death. St Edward's church provides a contrast with its well-maintained appearance.

Pirbright – The name Pirbright comes from *Perifrith*, a corruption of two old words meaning 'pear tree' and 'wood'. The wrought-iron sign on the Green, bearing both names, was erected to commemorate the Queen's Silver Jubilee in 1977.

REFRESHMENTS:
The Cricketers Inn, Pirbright.
The White Hart Inn, Pirbright.
The Shop on the Green: coffees and teas daily except Sunday.

Walk 54   GOMSHALL AND SUTTON ABINGER $4\frac{1}{2}$m ($7\frac{1}{4}$km)

Maps: OS Sheets Landranger 187; Pathfinder 1226.
An open-country walk with good views of the North Downs.
Start: At 089478, Gomshall Station.

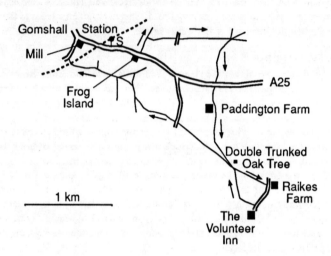

Leave the station through the gateway on the Guildford-bound side, and walk down to a road. Turn left, and at the Frog Island vegetarian restaurant, turn left again into a lane. After 150 yards, go right up a narrow path that leads into an area of woodland. Go over a stile to reach open grassland and continue ahead, walking parallel with the Downs.

After $\frac{1}{2}$ mile ($\frac{3}{4}$km) and a modest ascent, you will come to a triangle of open grassland: turn sharp right here to reach a gate after 50 yards. Go through and take the path running along the upper side of the field beyond. Go through another gate and descend through a gully to reach the main A25 road.

Cross the road with great care and continue along the bridleway opposite, a way that, in reality, is a concrete farm drive. Pass between the houses of Paddington Farm and then ascend on a track. At the top, 75 yards beyond a pole carrying overhead lines, there is a double-trunked oak tree. Turn left here and go through the hedgerow ahead. Now cross two fields diagonally to reach a road opposite Raikes Farm. Go right down the road to find the Volunteer Inn at the bottom.

Retrace your steps for 50 yards from the inn and take the bridleway to the left. This leads past the gate to 'The Shieling' and back to the double-trunked oak seen earlier. Now keep to the left of the hedgerow and follow the poles over the crest and diagonally down across two fields. Walk past a Woodland Trust copse and continue to reach a road.

Cross and continue up the track opposite to reach a field. Go half-way across the field, and, at the trees, bear half-right to exit through a gap lower down. Follow the lane beyond downhill for 50 yards, then go over a stile to the left. Cross the grassland beyond, continuing past Southbrooks Farmhouse. Now turn right along a track, passing a pond at the foot of a meadow.

Leave the track at the bend just past the bungalow, 'Twiga Lodge', and take the second, narrower path to the right of the hedgerow, following it to reach a road. Turn right through a railway arch and go right again along Goose Green to reach **Gomshall Mill**. There, cross the Tillingbourne and turn right, crossing the main road with care, to return to the station by way of the approach road.

POINTS OF INTEREST:
Gomshall Mill – This is an 11th century working water mill set on the Tillingbourne. It now comprises a restaurant, tea-room and shops. The mill pond, which provided the power to drive the larger, 18 ft diameter wheel, has been converted into gardens overlooking the river. Tel: 0486 412433.

REFRESHMENTS:
The Volunteer Inn, Sutton Abinger.
The Compasses Inn, Gomshall.
The restaurant and tea-rooms at Gomshall Mill are open from 9.30 am until 5.30 pm.

Walk 55   NORMANDY AND ASH   4¹/₂m (7¹/₄km)

Maps: OS Sheets Landranger 186; Pathfinder 1205.

A varied walk through fields, along country lanes and tracks, and over heathland beside Ministry of Defence firing ranges!
Start: At 926516, the car park on the A323.

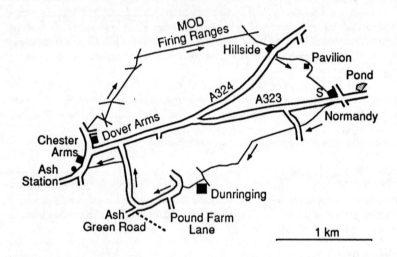

The starting car park is at the junction of Guildford Road (the A323) and Hunts Hill Road, **Normandy**.

Walk along the main road, with care, to reach the filling station and turn left immediately beyond it, going over a tubular stile. Cross the grassland beyond, exiting to the left of a house to reach a road. Turn right to reach the front of the house, then take the footpath opposite. Beyond the gardens, keep ahead across a field and then veer half-left into the trees at the corner.

Cross a plank bridge and stile, and head for the right corner beside the wood. Keep the trees on your left to reach an embankment, then turn right and walk for just less than 50 yards to reach a track on the left. Take this and walk to a T-junction. Turn left, then right to pass a house called Dunringing.

At the road beyond, turn left up a rise. Keep right at the junction with Pound Farm Lane, and at the bend by a metal mast, you will reach the railway. Do not cross the bridge into Ash Green Road: instead, continue ahead to reach a line of houses at the top of a rise. Now turn left along the path past Pine Cottages and head for the spire of St Peter's parish church, Ash. This church, dating from the 12th century, is not actually on the route of the walk, but is a useful waymark.

The path reaches the main road by the level crossing at Ash Station. Turn right, with care, and walk to a mini-roundabout. There, bear left up Ash Hill Road. At the first turning on the right, Fox Hills Lane, take the path by the road name board climbing up to reach overhead lines. Turn right there to go along the clearing.

You will soon reach a diagonal crossing track: go half-left into the wood on a concrete slab path which rises to meet a track. Now keep ahead to pass through a clearing surrounded by tall conifers. At the junction, with a triangular Army warning notice, go ahead to reach a pole barrier and vehicle-entry prohibited sign. Here, turn right, following the fencing on a straight, undulating path which at two points crosses trenches.

At the flag-pole beyond the last major crest, you will meet a crossing track, barred to the left. Turn right here to reach a service road at the rear of some hoses. Go left to reach the road beside 'Hillside'. Cross and go down the stepped path opposite to reach a sports pavilion car park. Go clockwise around a quarter of the field, and then take the path leading to the football pitch, children's swings and tennis courts. The starting car park is a short distance beyond.

POINTS OF INTEREST:
Normandy – A stroll around Normandy Pond should not be missed. Completely hidden from the road, it is reached via a woodland path marked by a white-topped post near the entrance to the Royal British Legion Club. The pond had been almost forgotten since the turn of the century and had become overgrown and silted up, but in 1987 it received the attention that has brought about today's pleasant spectacle.

REFRESHMENTS:
The Chester Arms, Ash.
The Dover Arms, Ash.

Walk 56   RICHMOND PARK   4³/₄m (7³/₄km)

Maps: OS Sheets Landranger 176; Pathfinder 1174 and 1175.
A walk in the park, with deer for company.
Start: At 193706, Kingston Gate car park.

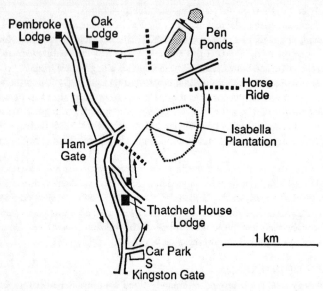

Thousands of motorists each day experience the tranquillity of Richmond Park as they drive around the 6¹/₂ miles of perimeter road in between the six vehicle access gates: Kingston, Robin Hood, Roehampton, East Sheen, Richmond, and Ham. The walk described here takes you to places that cannot be reached in the car, but it nonetheless starts at the car park by Kingston Gate. The Park itself covers 2469 acres, and contains Thatched House Lodge, the residence of Sir Angus Ogilvy and his wife, HRH Princess Alexandra. Deer roam freely.

From the upper car park exit, cross the road and head up to the oak trees. At the top of the rise, bear left, keeping to the top edge of the slope to reach a drive leading to Thatched House Lodge: fork right to pass the wire fencing of the adjacent house. Follow a wide path through bracken, with aircraft regularly passing by in front on their approach into Heathrow. Go across a small bridge with brick parapets and fork left to reach a horse-ride. Continue across on a level path through the middle of the grassland to reach the fenced Isabella Plantation.

By the entrance, there is a general information board which also has a monthly bulletin detailing current points of interest: do read this. On it you will read that the possible derivation of the Plantation's name is from 'Isabell', meaning dingy yellow, referring to the colour of the clay topsoil, and that work to plant a stream-side walk started in 1950. The 17 hectare area was duly opened to the public in 1953. Explore thoroughly at your leisure: words cannot do justice to the area's charm and beauty, especially when there are few people about. Trees, shrubs, lily-ponds with water birds, and above all the flowering plants can be enjoyed from the gravel paths, whilst seats formed from old tree trunks offer shady rest opportunities.

After exploring, leave by the exit at the far end, and turn left around the boundary fence. Further round, the walk reaches a locked gate: this part of the plantation is not open to the public, so fork half-right and drop down to another horse-ride. Go forward to reach a paved roadway, well to the left of the car park, and maintain direction to reach the larger Pen Pond.

Walk around this anti-clockwise, picking your way between the swans, geese and ducks that frequent a particular area of the shore. At the end of the causeway between the two ponds, turn left, then fork half-right. Keep ahead over the next horse-ride to reach the perimeter road by Oak Lodge.

Cross over to the right to enter the grounds of **Pembroke Lodge** at the back of the car park. At the rear of the house, turn left through the gardens and exit by a gravel path leading off the bend.

Any of the paths ahead which run parallel with the road can be followed, but for the best of the views keep to the top of the hillside. Descend into a little valley just up from Ham Gate and follow the track inside the boundary wall to return to the start after another 15 minutes of walking.

POINTS OF INTEREST:
Pembroke Lodge – The Lodge was the boyhood home of the philosopher Bertrand Russell. A plaque inside the house explains that the property was a gift from Queen Victoria to his family.

REFRESHMENTS:
There is a café at Pembroke Lodge, inside the house and on the terrace.

Walk 57   WINKWORTH ARBORETUM   4³/₄m (7³/₄km)

Maps: OS Sheets Landranger 186; Pathfinder 1245, 1246, 1226 and 1225.

A good opportunity for unhurried exploration of Winkworth Arboretum occurs near the end of this walk from Hascombe.

Start: At 999398, Hascombe village fountain.

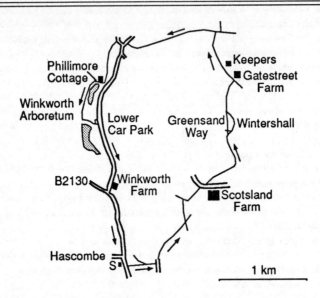

Take the grassy footpath opposite the fountain and head for the houses ahead. When you reach the paved roadway, turn left through gates on to the Greensand Way, which is followed for the whole outward route. At first the walk rises quite steeply to join a track coming in from the right. After the wooden barn, the track levels out. Go left at the crossing through an area of active forest management, then keep ahead on a narrower path. Turn right at a T-junction, dropping down in a gully, and bearing left to reach a road.

Turn right alongside the wall of Scotsland Farm, but only for 50 yards, though a closer peep at the buildings themselves is recommended. Go left up the bank and follow the path through a wood and then across open meadow. A stony track leads on to 'Wintershall', but on the bend, bear left up the steep grassy hillside and cross the track at the top.

The path descends diagonally to the bottom right corner: there, go left along the drive. Beyond the barn, keep to the field perimeter beside the wood to reach Gatestreet Farm. Turn left to pass 'Keepers', and maintain direction to reach an offset four-way junction. Here, leave the Greensand Way and turn left into a field, climbing straight up the centre, with the wire fence on your left. At the top, go through a newly tree-planted area, heading for the left-hand corner. The path continues to reach a stile, beyond which is an exhilarating area of upland pasture. Keep to the right edge across this, then descend, keeping to the right side of the grassy bowl with its solitary tree in the middle, to reach a stile just below a telegraph pole. Go over and continue down to reach a road. Turn left along the road (Thorncombe Street).

At the junction, turn right towards Godalming, then go left just beyond the stream. Cross a stile and keep to the left, going left again over another stile before the hillside rises. Proceed through a couple of fields to reach a drive and turn right to pass Phillimore Cottage. At a ground-level sign requesting 'Dogs on leads please' a few yards past the stile on the right, turn left to skirt the lake and enter **Winkworth Arboretum**. Spend as much time as you wish strolling around the grounds (the National Trust does ask for a donation towards the upkeep), then make your way to the lower car park, and turn right along the road. Bear left at the junction by Winkworth Farm to return to the fountain in the village.

POINTS OF INTEREST:

The fountain – The village fountain was built in 1877 by Edward Rowcliffe, a local man, in remembrance of his brother Henry. A plaque commemorates the Queen's silver jubilee exactly one hundred years later.

Winkworth Arboretum – The arboretum was the brainchild of Dr Wilfrid Fox, 1875-1962, who planted exotic trees and shrubs on this hillside site. Collections of maple, magnolia, birch, cherry, azalea and rhododendrons provide an astounding display of colours throughout the varying seasons of the year. The site, which includes two lakes, covers 97 acres and is now owned by the National Trust.

REFRESHMENTS:

Teas are available in the Arboretum.

Walk 58   NORBURY PARK   4³/₄m (7³/₄km)

Maps: OS Sheets Landranger 187; Pathfinder 1206.

Admire an imposing mansion from various angles, and enjoy its surrounding countryside.

Start: At 168518, Boxhill Station.

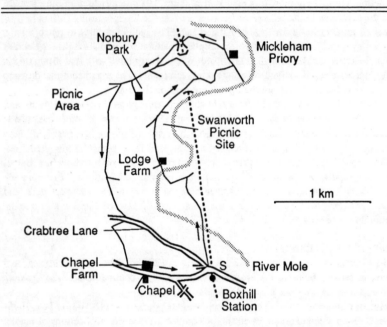

From the station, turn left over the bridge, then right down a path to a field. Stay beside the railway and cross the River Mole. Ignore the path under the arch, and make for the house to join a track. After walking about 150 yards along the track, turn left towards Lodge Farm on a roadway which bends to cross the river. Just before the farmhouse, turn left through a wooden gate and then walk alongside the stone wall.

Go through a gate, or over a stile, giving access to Swanworth Picnic Site, with picnic tables and benches provided. Beyond the site join a bridleway which climbs gently under the trees. A break in the foliage, and lucky timing, may give you the chance to watch a train emerge from or disappear into, the hillside beneath you. It is then only 100 yards to the brow of the hill.

Turn right down the roadway to reach a junction at the bottom, and turn left to pass Mickleham Priory and the farm buildings. Fork left along the raised track to reach a cottage nestling in a wood, and take the gated track going uphill through the trees. The track rises steadily, passing under the railway and going over at a crossing, to rejoin the road. Turn right to reach the gated entrance to the house in **Norbury Park**.

Continue on around the perimeter to reach a picnic area, where there is an information board, and follow the finger-post towards Westhumble, with the sawmill on your right.

At a fork, leave the road, which goes left downhill, and take the bridleway and cycle route ahead, staying at much the same level before descending into the Crabtree Lane car park. Turn right up the road for a few yards, then cross a stile into the field on the left. Go diagonally down the field to reach a stile half-way along the bottom boundary. Go over and drop down to a road. The view towards the spire of Ranmore church from here is delightful at any season of the year.

At the road, turn left to reach a ruined chapel and the entrance to **Chapel Farm**. Continue along the road, taking great care as there is no pavement. At the crossroads, follow Adlers Lane as far as the electricity enclosure, then turn left along the single-file path. Follow the path to the road and turn right for the station and the Stepping Stones Inn further on near the A24.

POINTS OF INTEREST:
The River Mole – The river rises in the vicinity of Gatwick Airport and flows into the Thames at East Molesey, opposite Hampton Court Palace.

Norbury Park – The Park was purchased by William Locke in 1774, and he commissioned the building of the present house. A subsequent owner was Leopold Salomons, who is remembered for his gift of Boxhill to the nation in 1914. Surrey County Council acquired the Park in 1931. The next year, the house, together with 40 acres of land, was sold, and it is still privately owned.

Chapel Farm – Through its numbered animal trails in farmyard and field, the farm offers visitors, particularly children, the opportunity to meet most farm and domestic animals at close quarters. Activities such as sheep-shearing and dipping can be watched and there is also a trailer ride which explores the more distant parts of the 200 acre farm.

The farm is open every day from mid-February until November, 10 am – 6 pm. Tel: 0306 882865.

REFRESHMENTS:
The Stepping Stones Inn, between Boxhill station and the A24.

Walk 59 PEASLAKE AND HOLMBURY ST MARY 4³/₄m (7³/₄km)

Maps: OS Sheets Landranger 187; Pathfinder 1226.
A village to village walk, with a pub in each one.
Start: At 086447, Peaslake village stores.

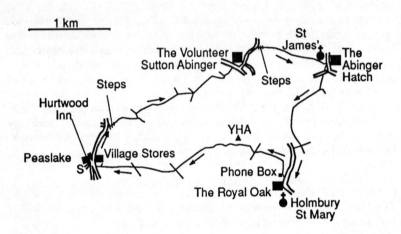

From the cross, walk along Peaslake Lane to the bend, then ascend the flight of steps beyond the metal barrier. At the top, go left across the grass, passing the swings, and continue on a path between fields to emerge at a lane. Turn left to reach a road, then go right after a few yards up the drive past 'Timbers Ridge'. Keep ahead on a path, go over a stile, and cross an undulating area of grassland. When you reach the trees, cross a stile and go down the left side. Climb up the opposite bank and go over another stile to join a drive. When this turns left by a telephone pole, go ahead up a path to reach a roadway. Turn left on this, going straight on down a hill between fields. On a left bend, turn sharp right to reach a gate and walk up the left side of the field beyond, exiting in the corner by going through a barrier. Turn left for a few yards, then take the path opposite 'Stile Cottage' and walk down to the Volunteer Inn in Sutton Abinger.

Continue up the road behind the inn, walking through a deep cutting. After 200 yards, climb the 37 steps on the right to reach a track leading away from a farm. Now, as you walk towards the houses of **Abinger Common**, there are pleasant views of the North Downs. Keep ahead to reach St James' church and walk through the lych gate. Cross the grass outside the churchyard wall towards the swings, go over the road and enter the field opposite by going up six steps. Walk straight across to the woods and drop down to meet a path running under overhead wires. Turn right to reach Holmbury St Mary. Walk past the first houses to be confronted by a gate and stile. Turn right beyond these to join a road and go left.

Just before the green, above which sits the church, turn up right by the telephone box. Climb quite steeply into woodland and then keep ahead on a broad path. Continue over a wide crossing track in a dip, to reach a pole barrier and concrete 'barrels' above the entrance to a Youth Hostel.

Maintain direction for 150 yards along the boundary fencing to your right to reach a metal gate. Take the narrow path directly in front, or the track which does an anti-clockwise loop to join it at a excavated bowl, which may be filled with water. Continue ahead, ignoring all turnings to left and right, of which there are several, and maintain a generally straight and level course to reach a roadway by 'Tor Cottage'. Go down the bank opposite, taking care, to return to the start.

POINTS OF INTEREST:
Abinger Common – To the side of the green, between the lych gate of St James' church and The Abinger Hatch, are the stocks.

REFRESHMENTS:
The Volunteer Inn, Sutton Abinger.
The Abinger Hatch, Abinger Common.
The Royal Oak, Holmbury St Mary.
The Hurtwood Inn, Peaslake.

Maps: OS Sheets Landranger 187; Pathfinder 1208.
A circuit, very near the Kent border, with views to the Weald.
Start: At 425518, the Carpenters Arms, Limpsfield Chart.

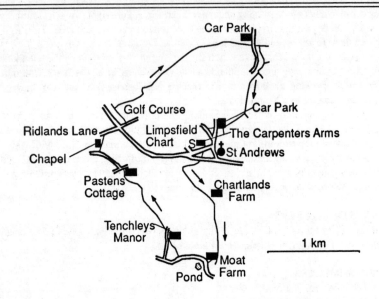

Take the path behind the bus shelter and cross the busy road with care. Continue towards 'The High', using the log-lined drive, and turn right in front of the house to drop down to 'Quince House'. Follow the path beside the stone wall, going down to reach a lane. Turn left, walking past 'Caxton House' to reach Chartlands Farm. There, go down the wide grass track beyond the metal gate and heed the footpath notice when it directs you into the left field. Cross the rising slope ahead to reach a stile. Go over and keep ahead to reach another. Go over and turn right towards the buildings, leaving the field at the entrance to 'The Old Lodge'.

Walk round the pond, go past Moat Farm, and continue along the road until you come to a footpath sign under overhead lines. Turn right here and walk to a farm drive reached beyond a bridge. Turn right to reach a pond, then go left to reach the grey silos. Now follow the edge of a field, walking beside the hedgerow. Keep left at a metal gate and ascend the grass hillside to reach the top left corner from where there is a very pleasant view. The spot is also an ideal rest opportunity, with trees for shade if required. Cross the stile in the corner and climb up the path beyond, which runs beside a paling fence. Near the top, you will reach a garden fence on the left: look out for a gate, go through it and turn right to follow a drive to the top, reaching **Pastens Cottage** on the right.

Go forward down the road to reach a bend and take the footpath just before the stone cottage. Go through a kissing gate and continue to reach the next road at Pains Hill chapel. Turn right and walk to the main road. Cross, with care, to reach Ridlands Lane and immediately turn left along a bridleway. Bear left after a few yards and bear left again further down to cross two fairways of a golf course. Turn right off the cinder track at the second of these, keeping the trees to your immediate left. Walk past the green, then follow a path to reach a stile leading into a field on the left. Half-way down the field, turn right into a wood. Continue across a field strip and then walk ahead at the edge of the woodland.

When you reach a meadow, go through a latched gate, exiting the field through a similar gate in the opposite left corner. After a further 75 yards, take a sandy path climbing to the right to reach a football pavilion at the top.

Go through the pavilion's parking area and cross the road beyond. Now walk along a gravel track, passing the High Chart name board. At a marker post a few yards beyond, turn right passing first through an area of newly planted trees, then entering a conifer wood. Turn right at the T-junction along the sunken path to approach a road. Turn left away from the gate, then go right after a few yards. Now follow the yellow arrowhead leftwards at the next post to reach a junction by the Askew memorial seat.

Here, take the path going right, behind the seat, and go past a pond. Fork left beyond this, rising to join a broad track. Go right, along the track, keeping ahead past the blue NT arrowheads at ground level, and then bear left at the next fork to reach a car parking area. Cross the road to the cricket pitch and turn left up the road to reach a junction. St Andrew's church is now ahead and to the left, and the inn at which the walk started is to the right.

POINTS OF INTEREST:
Pastens Cottage – On the cottage wall is a plaque recording the fact that Sergey Kravehinsky Stepniak (1852-1895), a Russian writer, lived there.

REFRESHMENTS:
The Carpenters Arms, Limpsfield Chart.
Joyces-on-the-Chart, Limpsfield Chart, for coffee and teas (closed Thursdays).

Walk 61   NEWDIGATE AND CAPEL   4³/₄m (7³/₄km)

Maps: OS sheets Landranger 187; Pathfinder 1226.
A level walk between two villages, both with pubs by the church!
Start: At 198420, St Peter's church, Newdigate.

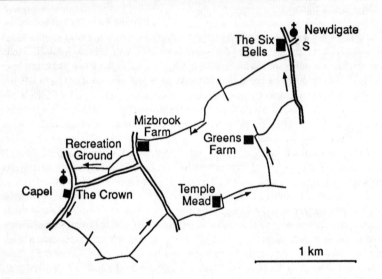

Walk down the street in the direction of Rusper for 100 yards and then take the footpath beside the last house on the right. Keep ahead from field to field using the stiles, to reach, in the far corner of the fourth field, a plank leading to a farm drive.

Carry on into the next field, keeping alongside the wood on the right. From the bottom corner, pass through the copse to reach a plank bridge. Cross to emerge into a clearing and follow a line of electricity poles to reach another plank bridge and a stile. Cross and keep left along the next field. Cross into the adjacent field at the end corner and maintain direction through the dip by the pond to reach a road at Mizbrook Farm.

Turn left to reach a bend and then go right along a drive. Bear left on to a path skirting two paddocks, then cross a bridge over a stream to enter a recreation ground. Leave the ground by going to the right of the pavilion at the top, and turn left along the main street of Capel to reach the church of St John the Baptist and the Crown Inn.

Continue through the village to reach the Methodist church and turn left at the green just beyond. Cross a stile and walk along the left hedgerow to enter the adjacent field. Now walk to the crest ahead and take a path through the meadow beyond to reach the far hedgerow. Cross here on one plank and re-cross to the left on two! Now keep to the left and then make for the central finger-post. There, bear left to reach a brown metal gate. Go through to enter a wood and keep ahead to reach a cottage and the road beyond it.

Turn right for 125 yards to reach the entrance to 'Temple Mead'. Now walk half-way along the drive to reach the brick pillars and go right through a gate into a field. Continue by walking parallel with the drive. By the house, swing left to reach a green gate just beyond the tennis court. Bear right here to reach and cross a field, keeping just to the right of the central hedgerow. A causeway now leads to a concrete bridge. Cross and, 50 yards further on, cross a stile and then a stream. Now climb to the left corner and head for the farm buildings.

In the farmyard, turn right in front of the brick barn to pass a pond. Go ahead over two stiles and through the lower gate to reach a road. Turn left along the road to return to the church.

POINTS OF INTEREST:
Capel – The almshouses in the village were erected in memory of Mr Charles Webb by his sons and daughters. An inscription recalls those days in the 1870s when Surrey included Clapham Common. Today, the county's connection with that general area of south London is the Oval, home of Surrey cricket.

REFRESHMENTS:
The Crown Inn, Capel.
The Six Bells, Newdigate.

Walk 62   BLETCHINGLEY AND SOUTH NUTFIELD   5m (8km)

Maps: OS Sheets Landranger 187; Pathfinder 1207 and 1227.

A level walk almost throughout, largely across fields.

Start: At 327507, the Whyte Harte, Bletchingley.

Cross the main road to the Parish Church and go through the churchyard keeping to the left. At the end of the surfaced footpath beyond, continue to the junction facing some steps and turn left. Cross the main road again, continuing down Castle Square past the site of the village pound, last used in 1899.

At the junction, take the footpath to Nutfield, which rises above the private road. The land falls steeply away to your left where a couple of houses and a lake (passed later in the walk) make for a very pleasing view, and seats carved out of a fallen tree, may tempt you into an early stop.

Having descended, you will reach a track coming from the gated field on your right. Go over the stile ahead and keep to the right edge of the field beyond to reach the motorway (the M23). This is passed by means of a tunnel. Follow the track ahead between the rounded hillocks to reach a road close to 'Hawkesbury'. Turn left and walk to the bend. Now drop down to the stile beside a gate leading into the private grounds of 'Kentwyns'. Keep to the left side of the field, exiting in the corner and continuing into South Nutfield.

Turn left along the street past the Village Hall, walking as far as the gravel drive opposite number 124. The Station Inn is 100 yards beyond the arch ahead, at the junction with The Avenue. Follow the drive to its end, beyond the Scout Hall, and bear half-right. Cross the railway tracks, which are dead-straight in both directions, by means of about 100 steps, then bear left to reach a road. Walk ahead on the drive to Crabhill House, a holiday home for the disabled run by the Winged Fellowship Trust, and turn left beyond it to cross the M23.

Follow the path ahead to reach a road and then take the bridleway past the red brick barn of Henhaw Farm. After 100 yards, opposite the house, turn left over a stile and cross two fields to reach the railway again. This time wooden staircases help the walker over the lines on to a track; walk ahead to pass the barn in the distance. Bear right at the fork, passing the lake seen earlier. At Castle Hill Farmhouse, go up the drive, and turn right at the top. The path leads to a road; turn left to return to **Bletchingley** and the start of the walk.

POINTS OF INTEREST:

Bletchingley – In the Middle Ages this was a town of some importance, being a centre for wool production. However, its population declined, and its two seats for Members of Parliament were abolished in 1832 under the Reform Act that did away with these 'rotten boroughs'. Nothing remains of the castle that once stood on Castle Hill.

REFRESHMENTS:
The Whyte Harte, Bletchingley.
The Prince Albert, Bletchingley.
The Red Lion, Bletchingley.
The Station Inn, South Nutfield.

Walks 63 & 64 ASHTEAD COMMON 5m (8km) or 8m (13km)
Maps: OS Sheets Landranger 187; Pathfinder 1190 and 1206.
A generally level walk by fields and woodland.
Start: At 179633, Chessington South Station.

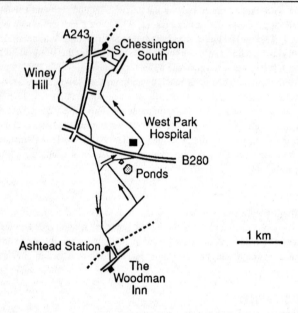

From the station, turn right to reach the main road (the A243). Cross and walk along
the lane as far as the entrance to Winey Hill, on the left. Climb up to the crest of the
hill and follow the ridge. At the far end of the ridge, drop down, passing six tree
stumps, and continuing beside the perimeter fence of the Chessington World of
Adventures. At the stile and signpost just before the wood, turn left and descend to
the main road. Cross with care and continue along the path opposite. This soon bears
right and becomes cindered as it heads towards a pylon. Here you cross a bridge over
the Bonesgate stream. Continue along the path beyond to reach a road by a war-time
pill box. Cross the road and take the path diagonally across grassland, heading for a
wood, where there is a white coal tax post (see Note to walk 44) and a notice board
about **Ashtead Common**.

126

For the shorter walk, turn left along the fringe of the woodland to reach the next Coal Tax post.

For the longer walk, continue ahead, going into the wood. Soon, bear slightly right, following the blue-topped posts. After a mile a concrete bridge with tubular railings is reached. For the easiest refreshment stop on the walk, continue ahead to Ashtead station, go over the level crossing and take the footpath behind the low brick buildings beyond the car park to reach the Woodman Inn. Retrace your steps to the bridge, then turn right through a barrier, walking parallel with the houses. When these end, at an opening to an avenue, continue ahead, bearing left to face a metal gate to private woodland. Turn right in front of this and continue through the wood to reach a crossing with the back of notice board ahead. Turn left up a grassy track. After 200 yards another crossing is reached, with a lone house to the left. Here, turn right for 35 yards, then go left along a firm path. Almost at the edge of the wood there is another coal tax post to the left. This is where the longer walk rejoins the short walk.

Go down the first path to the right to reach the **stew pond**. Walk around this anti-clockwise to reach, to the right, a flight of steps. Take these up to the **Great Pond**. Note that you <u>cannot</u> walk all the way around the shore. Return to the smaller pond, continuing the circuit of it, then turning right along the continuation of the path followed earlier, which is marked 'Winter Horseride'. After 250 yards the path reaches a road (the B280). Cross the road and follow the sign to Horton Lane to reach **West Park Hospital**. Take the path outside the right perimeter fence to reach a stile. Go over into a field, crossing it to reach a road at the bottom and going on to meet another by the gate to Park Farm. Turn left for 200 yards, then bear right along a path to reach a road. Keep ahead to the end of a golf course, then turn left at a signpost. At the next signpost go half-right, as directed, to reach a road. Turn left along the road to return to the station.

POINTS OF INTEREST:
Ashtead Common – This common covers 500 acres and was designated an Area of Special Scientific Interest in 1955. It is owned and managed by the Corporation of London.

Stew and Great Ponds – The two ponds were constructed as far back as the 12th century. The larger was only restored between 1975-9, after its dam had been breached in the middle of the last century. The smaller, or stew pond was used for fish rearing, but is now home for many water birds which nest among the bulrushes.

REFRESHMENTS:
The Woodman Inn, Ashtead.

Walks 65 & 66   SHAMLEY GREEN   5m (8km) or 8m (13km)
Maps: OS sheets Landranger 186 and 187; Pathfinder 1226.
A secluded walk with pleasant viewpoints.
Start: At 052448, Hurtwood Car Park 8.

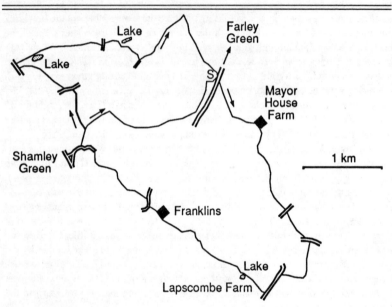

The car park is $^2/_3$ mile south-west of Farley Green, reached through gates at both
entrances. If the gates are locked, park on the nearby verges.

Cross the road and take the bridleway heading south-eastwards into woodland.
After $^1/_4$ mile, turn left at a path crossing, to reach Mayor House. Walk ahead, going
up a gentle rise to reach the start of a left bend. There, turn right over a stile and climb
up the right side of a field, going over a hill crest. In the next field, pass to the right of
a barn in a dip. Leave the field and walk along a path to reach a six-way junction.
Keep ahead on the track to Keepers Cottage, continuing on to reach a minor road.
Cross to reach a path heading in the same direction. Keep ahead at a path crossing,
going under overhead lines to reach another road. Turn left, soon reaching the entrance
to Hurtwood Car Park 5. Turn in here to enjoy the view. Now go down the steep path
ahead to reach a plank bridge. Cross and turn right, going right again on to a bridleway

which soon joins the drive from 'Alderbrook' and leads to a road. Turn left, and, at the foot of the hill, turn right into Lapscombe Farm. Pass between the two houses and bear left to reach a lake. At the T-junction at its second corner, go right and, after 150 yards, a second lake comes into view. Leave the track here, turning off left and going through a hedgerow. Immediately beyond, go right, following the top side of a field. In the far corner, join a track and follow it into woodland, and then past a small pond. Now walk uphill to reach a road. Continue uphill opposite to reach a gate and stile at the top of a rise. Go over the stile, turn towards a house, and leave the field by the stile facing the lake. Cross the grass half-right, following the direction of the GW arrowhead, and continue along the Greensand Way to reach a road. Walk forward to reach a path immediately on the left beyond Stroud Farm. Go across the foot of a sloping field and over a stile to reach a drive which leads away from 'Little Cucknells'. Just past the gate and name board, turn left. Continue along the drive to drop down past Reelhall Cottages to reach a road. Turn left into Shamley Green, but notice the entrance drive to Sandhurst Hill on the right, where the walk continues. Go up the narrow path to the left of the hedge beside the drive; the walks divide at the top by the house.

For the shorter walk, turn right, and exit the field over a stile. Follow the fencing to the top of the rise ahead, and then bear right to join a track. Stay ahead on this for $^3/_4$ mile to reach a gate beside a road. Do not go out on to the road; instead, turn left down the bridleway until you pass another gate into the private Albury Estate on the left. Now turn right to return to the car park.

For the longer walk, turn left and soon cross the fencing into the field, aiming for the house ahead and joining a track 100 yards past it. Continue to reach a road, by way of the path beyond the stile on the bend, and then turn left to the entrance of 'Tree Tops'. Take the path going up the bank. After emerging into grassland, go half-right towards the green dome of St John's Seminary, Wonersh $^1/_2$ mile away. Maintain direction across three fields and pass a cottage. Follow the hedge to the main road, reaching it with great care; there is no pavement! Turn right for 50 yards, then take the drive to 'Derryswood', on the right. Pass a cascade and 100 yards further on, go right through a gate. Go along a field and cross a stile just below a brick house. Keep ahead to reach a road and go along the drive to 'Darbyn's Brook'. At the end of the surfaced drive, go up a track to reach a road, and turn left. Go along for $^1/_2$ mile to reach a grass triangle by a cottage. Turn right, following a bridleway sign around the back of a garage. After 25 yards, under the overhead lines, go right up a narrow path. At the top of the trench section, turn left and gently climb back up to the start.

REFRESHMENTS:
The Red Lion Inn and *The Bricklayer's Arms*, both in Shamley Green.

Walk 67   FARTHINGDOWN AND HAPPY VALLEY   5m (8km)

Maps: OS Sheets Landranger 187; Pathfinder 1207.

*A walk combining views from a ridge, and the tranquillity of a
secluded and surprising, traffic-free valley.*

Start: At 308557, Chaldon church.

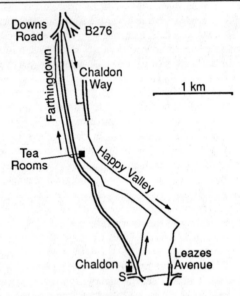

This is the longer of the walks starting from the church of St Peter and St Paul at
Chaldon. See Walk 21 for the shorter walk.

Walk down to the left of the triangle containing the sign bearing the past and
present spellings of Chaldon, and turn left along the road for 50 yards. Turn off right
into a field, heeding the notice that this is working farmland, and proceed over the
ridge crest, entering woodland on the far side. Descend for a few yards to reach a
finger post at the top of a wide valley, and turn left, maintaining this level.

The walk now reaches Devilsden Wood, maintaining direction as it rises to the
open ridge of **Farthingdown**, by some buildings. Cross the road and walk along the
wide grassland. At a pair of spreading trees, pass an ornate finger-post, with a sign for

Hooley, Coulsdon, Purley, and Chaldon. Keep ahead here, going gently down to reach the residential Downs Road.

Cross to the right side below the cattle grid, and return up the hill, taking the horse-ride, with the hedgerow on your immediate left. After $^2/_3$ mile (1,100 metres), look out for the finger-post just before a line of electricity poles commences; turn left as indicated and drop down to reach Chaldon Way. Turn right along the road and where it ends go forward along a path.

The walk is now following the pleasingly named Happy Valley, and will continue to its end where the walker meets a track. Turn right on this towards Leazes Avenue. Walk past the white railings and gate of 'Broadwood', continuing along the track to almost reach a road. Now turn right by the house, and follow the side of the field to a road. The church and starting point is just to the right from here.

POINTS OF INTEREST:

Farthingdown – Farthingdown, or Farthing Downs, has been owned by the Corporation of London for over 100 years. It was acquired to protect the area from residential development and to give Londoners somewhere they could enjoy fresh air and exercise. It is now proposed to introduce traditional grazing, and it is in connection with this that the new cattle grids have been placed at both ends of the road. The cattle grids have been designed so as to allow small mammals to escape should they become trapped underneath!

Walk 68   HASLEMERE AND GRAYSWOOD   5m (8km)

Maps: OS Sheets Landranger 186; Pathfinder 1245.
A varied walk with a modest hill-climb on the return section.
Start: At 904328, the Town Hall in High Street, Haslemere.

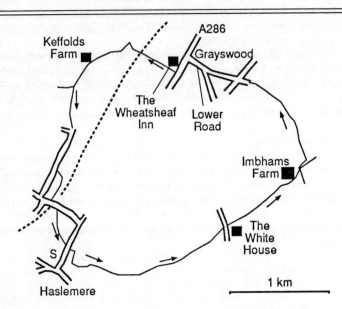

Walk along High Street to the Georgian Hotel and turn right into Well Lane. Follow the sign for Swan Barn Walk to enter a field. Beyond the barrier at its other side, turn left along a lane. After passing through a gate, go half-left off the track into woodland, crossing a stream. There is a circuit around Longmoor Wood ahead, but the walk continues to the right. Recross the stream, a headwater of the River Arun, and keep ahead, following its course, to leave the National Trust land of Witley Copse and Mariners Rewe. Cross a stile opposite Longacre to reach Holdfast Lane, continuing by taking the track ahead, past the White House.

Follow the track past some outbuildings of Imbhams Farm and on to where it runs beside a lake. At the bend beyond go left, then right just before the bungalow, going up the side of the field. Turn left through the gate after 100 yards, and cross the field to another gate. Keep ahead until the path goes diagonally towards a gap in a hedgerow. Go across the next field to join a track which emerges at a road junction.

Go ahead along Lower Road to reach the green at Grayswood and the main road (the A286). Turn left to reach the Wheatsheaf Inn and take the drive on the right just beyond. Descend on the path by the bungalow to cross a stream, then climb up to a railway embankment. Cross the tracks with care and drop down to reach a copse beyond a gate. The path now crosses a small pasture to reach a stile. Take the second path on the left, soon crossing a stream on a makeshift plank. As you ascend on the far side, a small lake comes into view on the right. Keep ahead at an old metal gate to reach the top of a holly-fringed gully. Now climb up the field heading towards the left of a house with an enviable view.

Follow the grassy path beside the stone wall and hedge to reach a finger-post by the gravel parking area. Turn left through a gate and keep ahead between the wooden fences to reach another, larger gate. Continue, to reach a fork, just past some tree stumps. Veer left and maintain direction to reach a road at the end of a muddy bridleway.

Follow the road through a housing estate to reach the end of a recreation ground. Turn left into The Spinney. Now go along the footpath between the fences to reach a road. Turn left over the bridge and then go right along Pathfields to return to High Street, reaching it just down from **Haslemere museum**, at the point where the **Greensand Way** starts or ends.

POINTS OF INTEREST:

Near to the start, you walk beside a charming stream which flows in a small valley smothered in spring with daffodils. This is a headwater of the River Arun on which the town of Arundel, with its famous castle, stands, and which reaches the sea at Littlehampton.

Haslemere Museum – The museum is open Tuesday to Saturdays between 10 am and 5 pm. Tel: 0428 642112.

The Greensand Way – This excellent walking route covers 55 miles from Haslemere to Limpsfield.

REFRESHMENTS:

The Wheatsheaf Inn, Grayswood.
All tastes are catered for in Haslemere.

Maps: OS Sheets Landranger 176; Pathfinder 1190.
A level stroll through parkland and by the Thames.
Start: At 178691, the Guildhall in High Street, Kingston.

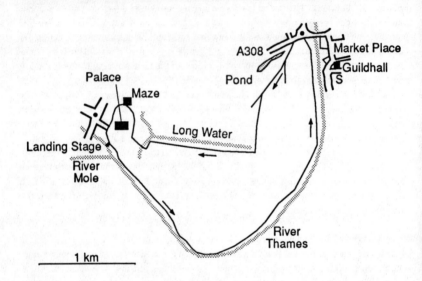

It seems appropriate to begin a walk from Kingston, the administrative headquarters of Surrey, though the start is at the Guildhall, not County Hall. The Guildhall, opened in July 1935, serves the Royal Borough of Kingston upon Thames, not the County Council. Beside it is the Coronation Stone.

Cross High Street to the Clattern Bridge over the Hogsmill and go through the gate and down the steps. The passage at the bottom leads to the entrance to Market Place. Turn left, and left again past Woolworths to reach the river. Walk along to the bridge and cross the Thames.

Enter Hampton Wick and follow the A308 left at the roundabout, passing the war memorial. At The Old King's Head, enter Hampton Court Park through the wooden gates and follow the drive beyond the cattle grid.

Bear right at the first fork, and left at the second. A notice here gives details of the plans to restore the avenues of lime trees, which were originally laid out in 1690. At the end of this avenue, the Palace is glimpsed above the embankment; head towards it on the far side of the Long Water.

About half way along, go off left to have a look at the Medieval Oak, believed to be over 1000 years old, then continue up to the railings guarding the Palace grounds. Turn left to enter through the gate and spend time enjoying the lawns, flower beds, trees and shrubs. There are charges for admission to the Palace and the famous Maze, but the gardens are free.

When you are ready to return to Kingston, go to the front of the building and walk through the gate to reach the riverbank. The landing stage is just downstream if you would like to take a boat back, but the walk along the pedestrian footpath is easy, with plenty of seats on which to relax and watch the river activity. Follow the bank all the way back to Kingston and cross the bridge, turning right to return to the Guildhall.

POINTS OF INTEREST:

The Coronation Stone – The stone beside the Guildhall, was, according to tradition, used during the ceremony of coronation by seven Saxon kings between 900 and 979.
Landing Stage – Just beyond the landing stage at Hampton Court, look over to the other bank to see the confluence of the River Mole with the Thames.

REFRESHMENTS:

The Bishop out of Residence, Kingston.
The Gazebo, Kingston.
There are a restaurant and a cafeteria in the grounds of Hampton Court Palace.

Maps: OS Sheets Landranger 187; Pathfinder 1227.
A level field-walk encountering quite a few stiles.
Start: At 224469, the Plough Inn, Leigh.

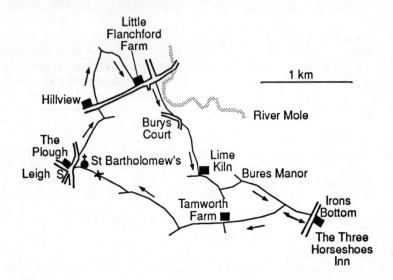

From the pump opposite the Inn, walk along the road past St Bartholomew's church, **Leigh**, to reach a bend. Now, just beyond the entrance to Willow Cottage, take the path through the gate on the right and cross the field beyond diagonally. In the next field, go over the ditch on the left, using planks, to reach a road.

Cross the road and continue along the track opposite, beside 'Hillview'. Go through a gate, beyond which the track leads into the first of two fields. At the end of the second, cross a double stile and turn right beside a hedgerow. Follow the yellow arrowheads to reach a path through trees and continue along it back to the road.

Turn left and pass the entrances of, firstly, Burys Court School and then Little Flanchford Farm. By the pole 20 yards past the farm drive, cross the stile in the hedgerow and follow the bank beyond to a wooden bridge. The River Mole is just to the left: follow it upstream to join a concrete drive.

Turn left along the drive and then fork left on a drive at the end of a brick building. The drive continues beyond the double gates, but then deteriorates to a stony track. When you reach a left bend, look over to your left to see the remains of an **old brick lime-kiln**, now almost hidden. Stay on the track, bearing left once the concrete recommences to join a tree-lined drive.

Within sight of a small bridge, you will come to a new metal footpath sign: turn right here. However, for refreshment, you may wish to continue 50 yards beyond the bridge and then to bear half-right across the field to reach the Three Horseshoes Inn at Irons Bottom.

Back at the sign, leave the drive and aim for a stile. Go over, cross the following two fields diagonally and continue towards a red brick and tile house at Tamworth Farm. At the covered entrance, cross the track, and the planks and stile in front, and maintain direction beyond the farmyard to go through a succession of fields.

At a crest, look for a stile in the hedgerow. Go over and bear right down the side of the next field, walking beside the trees. Go diagonally left across further fields to exit through a gate. Walk forward to join a wide grass path. Follow the path for 25 yards then, by an oak tree, cross the planks and a stile on the right, and walk clockwise around the edge of the field beyond to reach the far left corner. Turn left over a stile and go right to the hedgerow to cross a wooden bridge. Beyond the next field, an alley leads back into St Bartholomew's churchyard, though the church itself remains hidden until the last minute. Now take the short step back to the start.

POINTS OF INTEREST:

Leigh – The village name is pronounced *lie*. In the 15th century church of St Bartholomew are memorial plaques and a stained glass window commemorating members of the Charrington family, of brewing fame. They built and lived at Burys Court, which is passed on the walk.

Old brick lime-kiln – The kiln, now almost hidden to the left of the track, would have been used for burning chalk, quarried from the nearby North Downs. The result was lime, which improved the quality of clay soil. It was more economic to produce this near the fields than to transport it from the site of the quarry.

REFRESHMENTS:

The Plough Inn, Leigh.
The Three Horseshoes, Irons Bottom.

Walk 71   EWELL AND NONSUCH PARK   5¼m (8½km)

Maps: OS Sheets Landranger 187; Pathfinder 1191.
A level walk with associations with Henry the Eighth.
Start: At 226622, Ewell East Station.

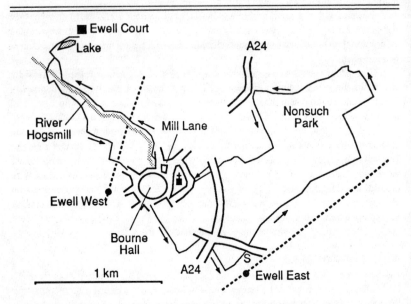

From the station, cross Cheam Road and turn into Nonsuch Court Avenue. Six local avenues are named after Henry VIII's wives, and it is Seymour that the route soon joins. At the top, enter a field and follow a path towards the distant spire in Cheam. At a T-junction in a dip, turn left. Cross two overgrown concrete roads and enter Nonsuch Park by going down a slope and turning right along the avenue. Beyond a barrier, turn left along the drive to the **Mansion**. At the front, immediately beyond the hedge, turn left and cross the grassland ahead to reach a car park. Here, turn left along an avenue to reach the **obelisks**. Beyond the third one, the avenue turns left. Do not go with it; instead walk ahead, going uphill on a surfaced path for 40 yards to reach the second crossing track. Turn right to reach a narrow concrete-slab path running parallel to the houses of Castle Avenue. When this path disappears, go half-right along a wider path to reach a low circular wall, the remains of Nonsuch Palace's Banqueting Hall. To the

138

left of the remains there is an expanse of grass; cross this to reach steps down to the busy A24. Cross with care and take the lane to the immediate left of the houses opposite to reach Ewell Castle school. Just beyond this, enter the churchyard on the right. Go past the old tower to the newer church of St Mary and leave by the lych gate. Cross 25 yards to the right, go down Mill Lane, and enter the grounds of Upper Mill. Cross the bridge with the brick parapet and turn right, following the stream and crossing two wooden bridges. Go through a tunnel under the railway, then turn right. Now go left along the riverbank to reach some stepping stones. Here, go half-right to reach the houses at the end of an avenue. Continue along the path for a further 40 yards and then go through the gate into the grounds of Ewell Court House. After a stroll around the lake, leave by the same gate and turn right. Continue along the surfaced path, crossing the Hogsmill river. Keep left for 40 yards, then take a path going left. When you emerge from the trees, walk ahead across grass, keeping a hedgerow to the right, to reach the end of a residential avenue. Walk along this to reach a bridge and turn left, continuing up Eastcroft Road. Turn right at the top and, shortly, go left along an alley between Nos. 122 and 124. Cross over the railway and follow the lane beyond to reach a one-way system. Turn right against the traffic flow, then go left, following the boundary wall of Bourne Hall. Go ahead into Lyncroft Gardens, then along an alleyway. Cross the next road and walk along a tree-lined avenue to reach Ewell High Street. Continue ahead, going along Reigate Road for 100 yards, before turning left beyond No. 17. Follow the path to its end and turn right up Cheam Road to reach the A24. Cross at the right hand side and go up the track opposite. Just before the house, turn left into an avenue and follow this back to the station.

POINTS OF INTEREST:

Mansion – The Mansion House in Nonsuch Park was constructed in 1802-1806. The service wing, with kitchen, sculleries, larders and laundries, has been restored, and is open to the public occasionally.

Obelisks – Nonsuch Palace was built by Henry VIII between 1538 and 1547. It was demolished in 1682 and only the three obelisks bear witness today.

REFRESHMENTS:
The Wheatsheaf, Ewell.
The Spring Tavern, Ewell.
The Green Man, Ewell.

Walk 72 PITCH HILL AND HOLMBURY HILL 5¼m (8½km)

Maps: OS Sheets Landranger 187; Pathfinder 1226.

An energetic walk involving ascents and descents of both hills.

Start: At 090409, the Bull's Head Inn, Ewhurst.

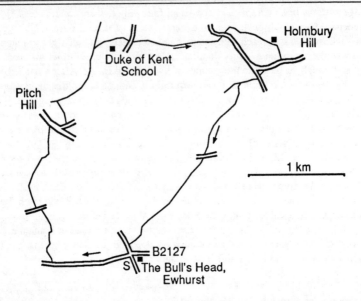

From the Bull's Head Inn, cross to the petrol pumps and go along the lane beside them. After around 10 minutes of walking a bridge with small brick parapets is reached. About 25 yards beyond, go right and climb up beside the edge of a field to reach a stile by a green metal gate. Turn left here, then right up the gravel drive to reach 'Rapsley' and a bridleway. Go up the bridleway to reach a road.

Turn sharp right along the road, then go left and uphill, past a letter box set in a brick column. After 125 yards, go left at the public footpath sign, climbing steeply to reach the top of Pitch Hill; there is a triangulation pillar at the main viewpoint.

Take the sandy path behind the pillar going directly away from the view, and very shortly fork right. Keep ahead past another vantage point where there is a metal seat, and continue at much the same level for 400 yards to reach a crossing track. Turn down right, then bear left on to a wide bridleway. When a marker post is reached, turn right, following the yellow arrowhead marked GW, the Greensand Way. Follow the Way as it descends to pass through the grounds of the Duke of Kent school and out on to a road.

The path continues opposite and just to the left, crossing the valley towards **Holmbury Hill**; there are clear markings at all junctions. When a road is reached, cross and go through the metal gate into Hurtwood Control Car Park 1. Take the wide path just to the right of the contribution pillar. Soon, go half-right through the concrete 'barrels'. Now, by taking any path to the right you will reach the top of Holmbury Hill, with its cairn and seat in memory of Reginald and Jocelyn Bray.

From the memorial go towards the scarp slope down the grass 'finger'. This finger becomes a path which soon descends very steeply to reach a road. Turn right past the cottages and walk to the end of a brick wall on the left. Now take the path to be found immediately to the left of a white gate marked 'Wayfarers'. At the end of the path a wooden staircase leads down to a road. Cross slightly to the left, and then proceed down the drive to Radnor House.

At the low brick building, walk ahead on a concrete path, then veer half-left by the pond beside a gatepost marked 'Private'. Just past the top of a rise, go left over a stile and cross a series of fields linked by stiles to reach a stony track. Now, walk ahead, passing some barns over to the right. A concrete bridge is used to cross a stream, after which you make for a gate in the woodland ahead. Beyond this a crossing track is reached; keep ahead, following the yellow paint daubs and arrowheads to reach a road. Turn left to return to the start.

POINTS OF INTEREST:
Pitch and Holmbury Hills – The hills lie to the west of the better known, and rather higher, Leith Hill. They both offer fine views as a reward for the effort in reaching the tops, at 843 feet (257 metres) and 857 feet (261 metres) respectively.

REFRESHMENTS:
The Bull's Head Inn, Ewhurst.

Walk 73 ALFOLD AND THE WEY AND ARUN CANAL 5¼m (8½km)

Maps: OS Sheets Landranger 186; Pathfinder 1246.

A walk to discover a long-abandoned canal.

Start: At 027351, Sidney Wood car park, off Dunsfold Road, near Alfold.

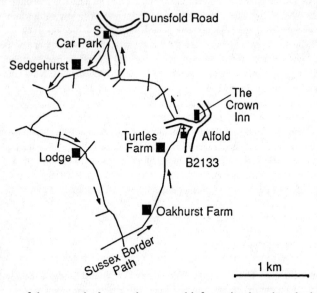

Leave the rear of the car park close to the covered information board, and take the 'Forest Walk', indicated by a pointer at ground level. The walk meanders through the wood, following numerous white-topped posts, to reach a barrier. Pass this to emerge on to a forest road. Turn right to the crossing at the corner of the 'Sedgehurst' paddock and go ahead through more barriers.

The path curves left to reach a seat: less than 100 yards beyond this, look out for the bed of the old canal, and climb up left on to the raised embankment running along the other side. The embankment used to be the towpath: stay on it to reach a track, set back from which is a large house, currently painted grey and cream, and protected by large-mesh fencing.

Turn left here, and keep ahead to reach the lodge at the far end. You will now

142

have left the Forestry Commission's Chiddingfold Forest. Turn right along the road into Sidney Wood Farm for a few yards, then continue left along the bridleway to rejoin the canal.

Maintain direction through three gates and across a bridge with tubular railings. Now walk ahead along a muddy track to reach a junction with the Sussex Border Path. Turn left to reach a gate that gives access to grassland, beyond which lies Oakhurst Farm. Leave the farm along the drive, with the spire of Alfold church, your next destination, straight ahead. Leave the Sussex Border Path just around the first bend, going left through a gate. Cross three fields, crossing stiles between them, and pass through a belt of trees. Now skirt the tennis court of Turtles Farm and resume your bee-line for the church, going over a stile at the corner of the sandy horse exercise ring.

When you reach the road at the end of the driveway into the cemetery, the village church and inn and a collection of picturesque cottages are to the right. However, the walk continues left, going along the road to reach a bend. Just past 'Bucklands' with its wrought-iron gates and gravel approach, take the path on the right. Cross two fields to reach a farm drive and continue across towards the red building. Change direction slightly in the next field to pass a corrugated barn and enter the wood ahead.

At the crossing, turn right for 10 yards, then left through the slanting barriers and right again at once. Now keep ahead, walking up to reach a stile. Pass down the left side of the field to reach a plank in the corner which leads to a woodland path. Follow the path to its end, which is at the entrance to the car park.

POINTS OF INTEREST:

Canal – The Wey and Arun canal was constructed during the Napoleonic Wars, between 1813 and 1816. It unfortunately had only limited use, carrying coal, chalk and farm produce, and closed in 1871. However, in 1970, the Wey and Arun Canal Trust was set up to restore sections of the route. So far, a number of bridges have been rebuilt, locks restored, and several miles of the canal bed cleared and dredged. The sections covered on this walk have yet to receive attention. The Trust is based at 24, Griffiths Avenue, Lancing, West Sussex BN15 OHW.

The Wey-South path is a 36 mile route between Guildford and Amberley, which follows parts of the old canal wherever possible, and also other paths where no towpath or rights of way exist.

REFRESHMENTS:
The Crown Inn, Alfold.

Walk 74 THE DEVIL'S JUMPS AND FRENSHAM PONDS $5^{1}/_{4}$m ($8^{1}/_{2}$km)

Maps: OS Sheets Landranger 186; Pathfinder 1225 and 1245.

An ascent of one of The Devil's Jumps, and a walk around Frensham Little Pond.

Start: At 858418, Frensham Little Pond car park.

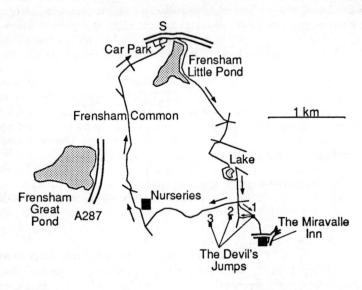

From the car park, commence a clockwise walk around **Frensham Little Pond**. After $^{1}/_{2}$ mile, the path leaves the waterside and reaches a fenced nursery on the left. Stay alongside the fence, continuing to reach the far end of the path through a concrete barrier.

At the junction, take the turning to the right, going alongside a garden fence to reach a road. Turn right along the road for a few yards, then go left into woodland by going between the poles and the stone wall. Continue ahead, away from the road. After 150 yards the track turns sharp left: about 200 yards further on, turn right at the first crossing track.

Walk to reach a small lake surrounded by rhododendrons but, alas, sometimes lacking water. Walk anti-clockwise around the lake: the path could well be rather

144

overgrown. At the clump of conifers, turn off right to join a sandy bridleway towards the three **Devil's Jumps**. Climb to the top of the left-hand hill by keeping ahead at the end of the sandy track. There is a fine all-round view from the top, with the lake you have walked around clearly visible. For refreshment, turn left just before the rocky summit and swing right descending to reach a road and the Miravalle Inn (previously called the Pride of the Valley).

To continue from the summit, go to the side facing the other Jumps and take the path down, turning right on to a track at the bottom. At a fork, veer left, following the grassy slope of the middle Jump, and continuing along the bridleway for almost a mile, to reach a road. Turn right, passing a nursery, and join a sandy path ascending to the National Trust sign for Frensham Common.

Take the bridleway in front, but to the right, which ascends to a ridge. **Frensham Great Pond** will come into view back on the left, followed by a resighting of the Little Pond to the right. Follow the ridge by either of the paths to reach a viewpoint with a seat. Carry on along the right-hand track which soon descends. Just after entering woodland, veer slightly right and, beyond a crossing track, go uphill to find the Little Pond below on your right. You will soon descend quite steeply: turn left to return to the car park.

POINTS OF INTEREST:

Frensham Ponds – The two ponds at Frensham, Great and Little, were created in the 13th century in order to provide fish for the Bishops of Winchester, who had a residence at Farnham. During the Second World War, both ponds were drained in order to prevent German bombers using them as a point of identification.

Today, the Great Pond is a popular sailing venue, and the coloured sails of the yachts, seen from the ridge, make a most attractive sight. The Little Pond, with its reedy inlets, and sandy coves and beaches, is more tranquil.

The Devil's Jumps – The story goes that the Devil, making his way to Churt from his Hindhead Punch Bowl by means of leaping from hill to hill, was knocked out by a stone thrown by the giant, Thor, who lived at nearby Thursley (Thor's lea). The hill climbed on this walk, the only one of the three that is accessible to the public, is named Stony Jump.

REFRESHMENTS:
The Miravalle Inn, Churt.

Walk 75   SHERE AND ALBURY HEATH $5\frac{1}{4}$m ($8\frac{1}{2}$km)

Maps: OS Sheets Landranger 187 and 186; Pathfinder 1226.

A favourite walking area south-west of Shere which, in many opinions, is the most attractive of Surrey villages.

Start: At 073478, The Square, Shere.

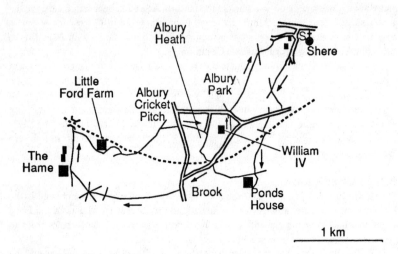

Walk up the road past the village inns and the **Museum**, and turn right into Pathfields. Beyond Number 19, go ahead on a footpath which rises into woodland. At a crossing, bear left and approach a road. Turn right between two gates and wind down to another crossing. Turn left to reach, and cross the road. The bridleway beyond takes you to a level crossing. Go over, and on the other side turn right to pass a line of cottages.

Keep ahead to reach the gravel drive of Ponds House. There, cross the stile on the right and follow the lane beyond almost to the railway bridge. Turn left along Brook Lane to reach the junction with Brook Hill.

Turn left for 50 yards, then take the track on the right, passing Brook Farm Stables. Maintain direction, leaving the track on the bend, and heading for the wood on the skyline. You will notice St Martha's Hill and church to your right.

Inside the wood, follow the path through the break in the conifer plantation and keep ahead at the end, going over a crossing marked with a 235 post. Continue to enter a wide clearing where heather flourishes, the hub of seven paths. Exit by the broad track in the far right corner, the track soon descending to reach a lane by 'The Hame' and a couple of other cottages.

Carry on down to reach a bridge over a stream, and 50 yards further on turn right over a stile. Cross the pasture beyond to reach fish breeding ponds and Little Ford Farm. Take the drive beyond the gate, walking past a new cottage.

At a T-junction, turn left and pass through the railway arch. Now rise gently in a cutting and, near the top, notice a sand pit on the left: within 50 yards fork right to reach Albury cricket pitch. Go forward to reach a road at the 'Woodside' post and continue opposite to reach an area of experimental **turf stripping**. Turn right at the bottom to go along the unmade Heath Lane. Continue to a red brick out-building. Turn left, and at the cottage with a weather vane midway along its roof, fork left on a path to reach a road.

Turn left along Little London to the William the IVth Inn, and continue on the track to the left of the road, walking up to 'South Lodge'. Take the footpath through the gate, and follow a line of massive chestnut trees. At the foot of the long slope you will reach a cottage situated just above a ford and footbridge. Do not cross the stream: instead, take the path along the bank to return to Shere, your final steps on this walk guided by the church spire.

POINTS OF INTEREST:

Museum – Shere Museum (telephone 0486 413245) contains nostalgic items from bygone days. It is open between Easter and September on Sundays and Bank Holidays 11 am – 7 pm, and Monday, Tuesday, Thursday, and Friday 1 pm – 6 pm. There is a small admission fee.

Turf stripping – This involves removing the grass which has invaded and covered the heathland in the time since regular grazing and fuel cutting ceased last century. Heather seeds can survive in the soil for at least 80 years, so it is hoped that with experimental treatment and management (such as removal of the turf) areas will revert to the old heathland state.

REFRESHMENTS:
The William the IVth, Little London.
The White Horse, Shere.
The Prince of Wales, Shere.
Aster's Tea Shop, Shere.

Walk 76 FRIDAY STREET AND LEITH HILL 5¼m (8½km)

Maps: OS Sheets Landranger 187; Pathfinder 1226.

A much-used route to Surrey's highest point, and a waterfall on the return.

Start: At 128456, the Stephan Langton Inn, Friday Street.

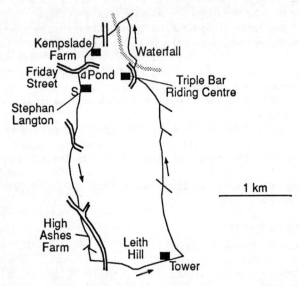

The **Stephan Langton Inn** is located in the cluster of houses beyond the head of the **pond**: walk up the lane beyond it, go through the barrier and into woodland. Just beyond a curiously large wooden bridge spanning a mini-stream, you will reach a road. Go left, then keep straight ahead on the bridleway by the letter box set in the wall outside the delightful 'Green Pastures'.

A further ascent follows through more pleasant woodland. At a fork, by a telephone pole, bear right, soon crossing the drive leading to 'Cherry Tree Cottage'. Now continue to reach a road. Turn left and when you reach a junction, take the road towards Ockley. Turn off the road when you reach a track leading to 'High Ashes Farm'. Keep ahead, ignoring the right turn to the farm itself, and also two subsequent side paths. At the T-junction facing a wooden gate, turn left to reach a road by a car parking area. Go across and follow the 'walker' finger-post for $^3/_4$ mile to reach the tower on top of **Leith Hill**.

Continue the walk by taking the steep path down the other side from the tower, going in the direction of the Landslip car park and Coldharbour Common, to reach a five-way junction at the entrance to The Dukes Warren. Turn left down a gated bridleway, following it, and the track which continues beyond another barrier, all the way to a road by the 'Triple Bar Riding Centre'.

Turn right and immediately follow a footpath down a lane through the private Wotton Estate. Cross a stream, the infant Tillingbourne just starting out on its journey to join the Wey at Shalford, and then walk past a waterfall and pool, regrettably not accessible and, indeed, fenced off.

Carry on along the track to pass a house and, 50 yards past its entrance drive, go over a stile on the left. Cross the grassland beyond, and an embankment, before climbing up a steep slope to reach a minor road. Keep ahead on the path beside a wood into a dip, and turn left there to pass behind a wooden stable. Now descend through trees to reach the entrance to Kempslade Farm. Turn right along the drive and continue downhill at the road to return to the start in Friday Street.

POINTS OF INTEREST:

Stephan Langton Inn – The inn is named after an Archbishop of Canterbury who was instrumental in forcing King John to sign the Magna Carta in 1215.

Pond – The pond at Friday Street was created by damming one of the streams feeding the Tillingbourne, originally for the purpose of driving a mill.

Leith Hill Tower – Leith Hill is the highest point in south-east England at 965 feet (294 metres). The tower was built by Richard Hull in 1766, and he is actually buried underneath it! The structure, which raises you to 1029 feet, was presented to the National Trust in October 1923 by a Reigate resident, Mr W J MacAndrew.

REFRESHMENTS:

The Stephan Langton Inn, Friday Street.

There is a teahouse at Leith Hill Tower when the tower is open (Wednesdays: 2 pm – 5 pm: Saturdays, Sundays and Bank Holiday Mondays: 11 am – 5 pm).

Walk 77   **CHIDDINGFOLD**   5$^1/_2$m (8$^3/_4$km)

Maps: OS Sheets Landranger 186; Pathfinder 1245.

A varied walk with modest ascents, early views into Sussex and the chance to make friends with some animals!

Start: At 961354, St Mary's Church, Chiddingfold.

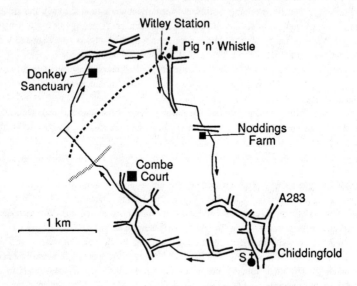

From the church, take the Grayswood road, keeping to the left of the pond. Just around the first bend, go up the footpath, climbing alongside the cemetery to join a residential road. When this turns right, keep ahead along an alley to reach an expanse of grassland. Walk along the top side of this. The high ground in the distance over to the left is Blackdown, the highest point in Sussex.

After half a mile, having crossed a drive, you will reach a road; turn right, passing the entrance to Langhurst Manor. Go down the hill to reach a road junction; turn right again. After 200 yards, just around a bend, turn sharp left along the drive towards Combe Court. The drive climbs and curves round towards the house. As it does, look out for a stile on the left. Go over the stile and bear half right. Cross two fields to reach a stile at the edge of the woodland. Go over and follow the path as it drops down to reach a stream which is crossed by way of a quaint brick bridge. Beyond, the path rises to reach a railway line. Cross the line with great care. On the other side, beyond a field, woodland is entered; bear right at a junction and follow a path down to a wooden bridge over a stream.

Follow the track beyond the stream, passing the **Lockwood Donkey Sanctuary** to reach a road opposite a post box. Turn right, passing the telephone box at the edge of Sandhills Common, and, at a bend, keep ahead, following the footpath sign. At the road crossing by 'Inglewood', turn right and cross the railway line again, this time at the end of the platforms of Witley station. Go through the white gate in front and pass Lilac Cottage. Now, keep ahead to reach a grassy path between buildings. When a field is reached, go to the left of the tennis court and out on to a road.

Cross the road and take the footpath opposite. Beyond a wood more grassland is reached. Now aim half-left to reach bridge. Cross and walk ahead to reach a broad grass track leading from the farm. Turn left, and, just past the house, go up right and continue over the hill crest. Descend and cross a stream, and re-enter woodland. Climb gently ahead, going out of the wood to reach the brow of a hill where you are confronted by a line of bungalows. Pass to the right of these and drop down to reach a road. Go left, downhill, then turn right along Coxcombe Lane to return to the green.

POINTS OF INTEREST:

Lockwood Donkey Sanctuary – The sanctuary is home for life for elderly animals, the population currently numbering over 200. Some 150 donkeys make up the majority, at present, but there are also horses, sheep and goats, all spending their later years in tranquil surroundings. The public are most welcome, especially children, who might like to 'adopt' one of the animals. There is no charge for admission. Tel: 0428 682409.

REFRESHMENTS:

The Crown Inn, Chiddingfold.
The Pig'n' Whistle, in front of Witley Station.

Walk 78   GATTON   5¹/₂m (9km)

Maps: OS Sheets Landranger 187; Pathfinder 1207.
A walk mainly through fields and woodland.
Start: At 290533, the Feathers Inn, Merstham.

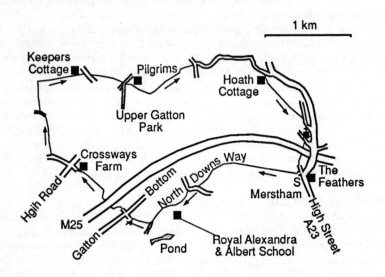

From the inn, cross the main road into Quality Street and turn left along the North Downs Way. Follow the National Trail past the cricket club and across fields to reach a road. Turn right and enter the grounds of the **Royal Alexandra and Albert School**. Bear right at the first fork, skirting the school buildings, and continue along the drive beyond to reach a road, Gatton Bottom. Cross the road and continue up the track opposite, passing under the M25 motorway.

Follow the track past Crossways Farm to reach a junction with High Road. Cross, and continue along Babylon Lane. After 200 yards turn right through a hedge towards the brick house of Gatwick Farm. Keep ahead past the barns, going into a dip, with a distant church spire pointing out the way ahead. Now turn right along a gated track, continuing ahead after the gate at the far end. At the very edge of a wood, cross into the field on the right and climb up to its crest. Keep ahead, going to the right-hand side of the fencing between the fields.

Go over three stiles to reach a road by Keepers Cottage. Cross and continue, going into and out of a dip, and walking across the grassland to reach a stile half-way along its far side. Go over the stile on to a road. The entrance to Upper Gatton Park (private) is to the right, but the route continues along the path beside 'Pilgrims'. Do not enter the wood at the stile; instead, continue on the grass, with the pink-painted mansion clearly visible over to the right.

Now keep ahead to reach an area of open woodland, smothered with bluebells in early spring. You emerge from the woodland and descend the left side of a sloping field, crossing into the adjacent field half-way down. At the road at the foot of this field, turn left to reach a junction. Go right, down a lane, passing a farm and descending to Hoath Cottage, which is within sight of the main road. The route does not go to the road; instead, take the path to the right and cross into the adjacent field beyond the swimming pool. Now aim for a point half-way along the field top and maintain this direction to reach a residential road. Go right, downhill to reach St Katharine's Church, its lychgate dated 1897.

Leave by either of the lower gates and cross the road to reach the North Downs Way by the entrance to Dell House. Cross the M25 again to return to **Quality Street**, admiring its interesting array of buildings as you return to the start.

POINTS OF INTEREST:
The Royal Alexandra and Albert School – The motto of the school, which stands in Gatton Park, is 'Nisi Dominus Frustra', which is derived from Psalm 127, Verse 1.
Quality Street – The street's name is said to derive from the play by J M Barrie because Sir Seymour Hicks, an actor, lived in the street whilst performing in the play.

REFRESHMENTS:
The Feathers, Merstham.

Walks 79 & 80 WISLEY RHS GARDEN AND OCKHAM MILL 5½m (8¾km)
or 7m (11¼km)

Maps: OS Sheets Landranger 187; Pathfinder 1190 and 1206.

Two easy walks, each offering a chance to visit the Royal Horticultural Society's renowned garden.

Start: At 067610, the Blue Anchor, High Road, Byfleet.

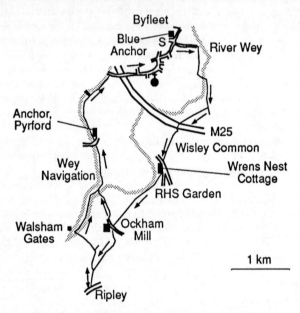

Cross to Clock House, and walk along its right wall, going past the four bollards. Walk along the road, Mill Lane, passing the nursery/garden centre, to reach the River Wey. Turn right in front of the bridge leading to Bluegates Hole. After something under ¼ mile, veer left on to a path and cross the river on a footbridge. Proceed to the top of a gentle rise beyond some buildings, and cross the stile on your right. Walk ahead towards the M25 motorway and cross over. Go down the steps on the left and turn right at the bottom. A few yards beyond the gate, bear left to enter the wooded seclusion of Wisley Common.

Keep ahead on the clear path which brings you to a road. Turn left for 50 yards to reach a fork. Keep ahead briefly on the concrete drive, then turn right over a stile by Wren's Nest Cottage. If you wish to visit the **Royal Horticultural Society Garden**, stay on the drive to reach the main entrance.

Beyond the stile, walk between fencing, which guards the garden to reach a drive leading into a golf club. Continue ahead along a track to reach the five-storey red-brick Ockham Mill, dated 1862. Having admired the cluster of buildings, and watched the rush of water entering the millpond, choose if you wish to do the short or longer walk.

For the shorter walk, follow the track to a gate and walk forward to reach the towpath of the Wey Navigation. Turn right here, rejoining the longer walk.

For the longer walk, go back along the road for about 100 yards and take the footpath on the right. Beyond the woodland, the path emerges on to a common. Keep ahead to reach a roadway, where the walk continues by turning right, but for refreshment turn left along the green into Ripley, where there is a selection of pubs.

Walk along the roadway, and after passing all the buildings, go left along a lane. Beyond Millstream Cottage and Oakbank, walk along a path to reach the Wey and the Navigation at Walsham Gates. These, like Worsfold Gates upstream, remain open except in times of flood. Pass the cottage and keep ahead along the towpath to rejoin the shorter walk.

After a mile, Pyrford Lock and The Anchor Inn are reached. Stay on the towpath as far as the second footbridge. There, turn away from the canal and follow a lane over the M25 and on to St Mary's church. Keep ahead along this residential road to reach the junction with Hart Road. Turn right to return to the Blue Anchor.

POINTS OF INTEREST:

The Royal Horticultural Society's Garden – This world-famous garden at **Wisley** is open to the public from 10 am, Mondays to Saturdays, but on Sundays is only open to RHS members. There is an admission charge. Tel: 0483 224234.

REFRESHMENTS:

The Blue Anchor, Byfleet.
The Anchor, Ripley.
The Ship, Ripley.
The Half Moon, Ripley.
The Talbot, Ripley.
The Anchor, Pyrford Lock.

Walk 81   **RANMORE AND WESTCOTT**   5$\frac{1}{2}$m (8$\frac{3}{4}$km)

Maps: OS Sheets Landranger 187; Pathfinder 1206 and 1226.

Save some breath for the climb near the end!

Start: At 146505, St Barnabas church, Ranmore.

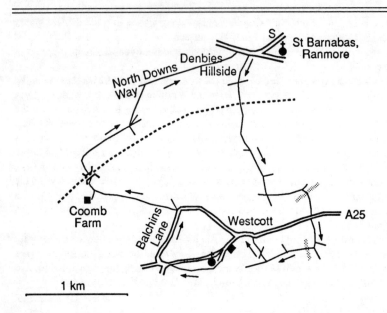

From **St Barnabas church**, walk along the road to the junction and the small group of houses that is Ranmore, and cross the grass to reach a stile by the red-brick cottages. The North Downs Way turns right at their rear, but you keep beside the wire fencing, making a steep descent, with one flight of steps, to reach a railway crossing. Go over and continue on the other side all the way to the corner by the first of the Westcott houses.

Turn left to reach the start of the second field and go right there over a footbridge. Now follow the lane from the house beyond to the A25. Cross, with care, into Milton Street and amongst all the pleasant cottages, look out for one on the right named Crooked Acre, which is linked to the road by a white-railed concrete bridge: take the wooden bridge just beyond it, under the weeping willow tree.

Ignore the first alley to the right, but take the second, which runs between long walls of brick and stone, and follow it to the centre of the village, where two of the pubs are to the right. The walk continues by going left to pass the third pub, and then climbing the hill leading to Holy Trinity church.

At the top of the hill take the sandy path on the right. Keep ahead past the houses and go over a roadway, following the yellow GW (Greensand Way) arrowheads to return to the A25 at the entrance to Rookery Drive.

Go over the brick bridge and turn off Coast Hill into Balchins Lane. Walk to the bend at the bottom and take the left-hand stile of the two flanking the gate. Go across four fields, the third and fourth of which are crossed diagonally to reach a small pond. Just past this, the walk reaches the buildings of **Coomb Farm**.

Here, turn right and head for the hillside. After the railway bridge, you reach a gate and turn right. A Forestry Commission sign has been placed at the next crossing: go half-left and left again following the red arrowhead.

Now climb up to the North Downs Way, marked with the official acorn logo, and turn right through a barrier. As you cross the grassy expanse of Denbies Hillside on the way back to St Barnabas Church and the start of the walk, look to the near range of hills: you should be able to pick out the tower on top of Leith Hill, the highest point not only in Surrey, but in the whole of south-east England.

POINTS OF INTEREST:

St Barnabas Church – The church spire, nearly 150 ft high, is a landmark for miles around, and will be seen from other walks described in this book. The church was built in 1859 to a design by the architect Sir George Gilbert Scott (1811-1878). Among his other notable works are London's Albert Memorial in Kensington Gardens, and St Pancras station.

Coomb Farm – At the farm you may be lucky enough to find Sarah Doney at work. She is a stonemason, and will be pleased to demonstrate her craft and to show you some of her output. Tel: 0306 889174.

REFRESHMENTS:

The Crown Inn, Westcott.
The Prince of Wales, Westcott.
The Cricketers Inn, Westcott.

Walk 82   HYDON HEATH AND HASCOMBE   5³/₄m (9¹/₄km)

Maps: OS Sheets Landranger 186; Pathfinder 1225, 1246 and 1245.

A walk, largely through woodland, which skirts Winkworth Arboretum, and visits the delightful Hascombe church.

Start: At 979402, Hydon's Ball car park off Salt Lane.

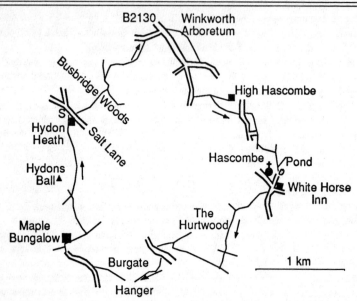

From the entrance to Hydon's Ball National Trust land, walk along **Salt Lane** in the direction of **Hascombe** for 50 yards, then turn left over a stile and go right down the stony track beyond. Just beyond the left bend, take the track forking right uphill, and continue ahead at the crest on the first bend. A short descent then brings you to a swathe of grassland between the trees. The cinder track beyond rises through badger territory to reach a drive.

Turn right at the top to reach the entrance to **Winkworth Arboretum**. Go into the car park, and take the path to the right of the house, marked 'No Access to Arboretum'. Walk to a road and turn right with care for 200 yards, then go left, passing the 'No Through Road' sign.

At the fork, bear left towards High Hascombe. Just before the white-painted lodge, bear right beside the high ivy-clad wall. Continue down a stony path to reach a road. Cross and go through the green gate. At a T-junction, turn right and pass a house. Beyond another green metal gate, keep ahead on a path for about 100 yards, then cross the stile on the left and head diagonally right across a field to rejoin the path beyond a shed. Go left to reach a drive and turn right, heading for St Peter's church whose spire comes into view.

Beyond the church and pond, you will reach the White Horse Inn. Cross the road and follow the finger-post to the gate and grass beyond. You are now on the Greensand Way. Climb to the wood and fork right after the stile, going right again after a stiff climb.

When you reach the crest, another marker post with a blue GW arrowhead points right. Do not follow it: instead, keep ahead. At the offset crossing, looking at first like a T-junction, turn right, then left, and turn right at the following T-junction to emerge from woodland to an expanse of bracken.

Walk to a broad track and turn left, passing a metal gate to reach a road. Go left for 100 yards, then right along a bridleway. On this walk along the slopes of Burgate Hanger, you enjoy wide views stretching away to the South Downs and Blackdown.

The path meets a lane: continue ahead up either since they rejoin at the top. Just past this upper junction, the Greensand Way turns off left. Do not follow it: instead, continue towards Maple Bungalow and turn right past the green gate. The sandy track ascends gently. Turn left at the gateposts towards the wooded hill. At the T-junction beyond the belt of trees, turn right along the wide track to return to the car park.

POINTS OF INTEREST:

Hascombe – The church of St Peter was built in 1864 and sits by the charming pond. Frequented by ducks, no doubt well-fed by the picnickers who take advantage of the seats, this pond and its surrounding green are a visual delight. Attractive cottages and a mini-garden containing a bird-bath, given in memory of the village school teacher, Daisy Coote, 1892-1978, complete a scene that will be long-remembered.

Winkworth Arboretum – The arboretum was the brainchild of Dr Wilfrid Fox, 1875-1962, who planted exotic trees and shrubs on this hillside site. Collections of maple, magnolia, birch, cherry, azalea and rhododendrons provide an astounding display of colours through the varying seasons of the year. The site, which includes two lakes, cover 97 acres and is now owned by the National Trust.

REFRESHMENTS:
The White Horse, Hascombe.

Walk 83   **PUTTENHAM AND CUTT MILL**   5³/₄m (9¹/₄km)

Maps: OS Sheets Landranger 186; Pathfinder 1225.

An undulating walk just south of The Hog's Back, using The North Downs Way for the return.

Start: At 931478, the Good Intent Inn, Puttenham.

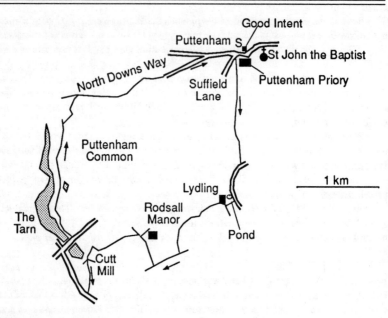

Walk along Suffield Lane, then go ahead over a stile just past the gateway of **Puttenham Priory**. Pass to the right of a semi-circle of four double columns and cross stiles to reach a field. At the far end of this, cross another stile and aim straight across the grass to the line of trees in the dip ahead. After another stile has been crossed the route drops down into a valley and joins a road beyond a metal gate. Go ahead on the road to reach a pond.

　　Turn right up the lane to pass 'Lydling' and continue ahead to reach a path. Ascend, and skirt an area of woodland on the right. The path now curls left under overhead lines to reach a crossing about ¹/₄ miles (400 metres) further on. Turn right, and, at the next marker post 350 yards down the hill, turn right again to reach the drive to Rodsall Manor. Follow the drive left, going away from the house, to reach the end of the stone wall. Just beyond, go ahead along a narrow bridleway and descend to Cutt Mill House.

Walk along the drive to reach a lake and turn up at the wooden posts to walk clockwise part of the way around it. With the sound of rushing water, the house set in its charming grounds, and the lake with its birds, this is a most picturesque spot.

Cross a stream, then a track, and go forward along the bridleway to reach a road. Turn right for 600 yards to reach a crossroads. Turn right again, passing the duck road sign! Their home, the lake on your left, is called The Tarn.

At the end of the causeway, turn left around the shoreline. The path veers away from the water to come to a junction with a three-stripe marker post. Turn left and walk to the next post at the top of the rise. Keep ahead to join a broad track beside the fencing on your left. Cross some planking and go past another pond. The path now rises gently beside tall conifers, then more steeply to emerge on to the openness of Puttenham Common, with The Hog's Back now visible in front.

The fencing is still to your left as you commence the descent, but you shortly fork right. Lower down, at the T-junction after a path has merged from the left, go left, and take any of the paths ahead to reach the North Downs Way, identified by the acorn logo. Turn right and walk along this well-trodden path to return to Puttenham and the start of the walk.

POINTS OF INTEREST:

Puttenham Priory – The Priory, described as a Palladian mansion, is privately owned and dates from the 1760s.

The adjacent churchyard (of the church of St John the Baptist) contains the village well. This apparently was last used in 1750, became forgotten, and only came to light again in 1972, when the covering collapsed into it!

REFRESHMENTS:
The Good Intent, Puttenham.

Walk 84   CHELSHAM   5³/₄m (9¹/₄km)

Maps: OS Sheets Landranger 187: Pathfinder 1207.
Pleasant valleys and a view of the London skyline.
Start: At 372590, the Bull Inn, Chelsham.

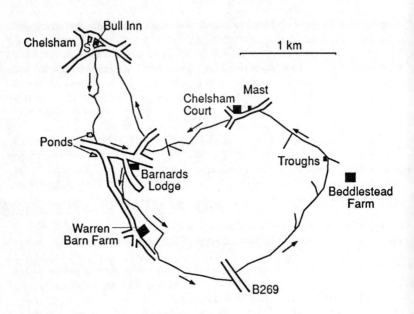

Cross the grass beyond the inn's car park to the Henley Wood name-board, turn left and walk to the last bungalow. Now take the finger-posted footpath, bearing right to reach two tubular gates at the end of the drive. Go through the left gate and keep beside the wood as you walk through two fields. In the recessed far right corner of the second field, cross a stile and bear left through a belt of trees into another field.

Pass under the electricity lines and go through a gap in the hedgerow. Now walk anti-clockwise around the field ahead to reach a little pond by the exit to a road. Turn left along the road (Limpsfield Road), going past a second pond on the other side, and walk as far as Barnards Lodge, the bungalow in the woodland. Go through the white gate and walk up the drive for 50 yards, then turn off right down a gravel path.

The path descends quite steeply to reach a road: go over a stile on to the hillside and continue beside the road to reach the fencing around Warren Barn Farm. Bear left above and away from the farm buildings to reach a gate. Now turn right over a stile and go forward to join the tree-lined track coming up from the farm. Turn left and ascend the valley to reach the busy B269, Croydon Road.

Turn left, with care, for 75 yards, then go right along the cart track. Proceed all the way across the field, with a slight kink in the middle, and, as you start to descend, ignore a left fork and swing round to enter the wood ahead through a gap in the trees.

Keep ahead on a grass path with the red roof of Beddlestead Farm (not on the route) coming into view in front. The grass path bears left, but you go forward down a short, steep path, soon crossing a stile. Descend half-left down the grassy slope beyond to reach a gate at the bottom, beyond the lone tree. Go through and continue to the left, walking along the valley floor and going through another gate to reach a group of three concrete troughs in a rough T-shape.

Go through the gate under the overhead lines and turn left along a track. You soon start to climb on a narrow path: inside the woodland, ignore a path to the left at a marker post, and continue the ascent to reach a road from where you have a fine view of the London skyline.

Turn left, passing the prominent mast, to reach a road junction. Go right and enter the field opposite the fencing below the drive to Chelsham Court. Now aim diagonally across four fields to reach a crossing just beyond a stile. Here, go ahead, between the two posts with red arrowheads, to reach a minor road. Turn right for 75 yards, then enter a field to the left at a red and white barrier, aiming for the tower of Warlingham Park Hospital. At the far end of the field go through a red metal gate to reach a road junction. Turn left along Chelsham Common Road to return to the start.

REFRESHMENTS:
The Bull Inn, Chelsham.

ELSTEAD AND TILFORD   6m (9½km)
or 8½m (13½km)

Maps: OS Sheets Landranger 186; Pathfinder 1225.
A walk beside stretches of the River Wey
Start: At 908437, the Woolpack Inn, Elstead.

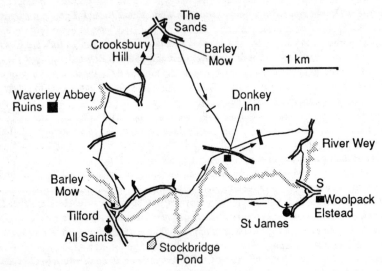

From the Woolpack Inn, walk along the Thursley road to St James Church, and turn
right into Westbrook Hill. When the metalled surface ends, turn right along a bridleway
into an Army training area. After ¼ mile there is a turning space on the right with four
tracks to the left. The one to Hankley Farm is private, so take either of the next two.
Walk past Upper Hankley Cottage, and after another 100 yards, veer right. Keep right
at the next fork, staying on the track above the River Wey. Pass a clearing on the left
and drop down to reach Stockbridge Pond. Continue along the track, with the pond on
your left, to reach the main road. Turn right, passing All Saints' church, to reach the
green at Tilford, close to the Barley Mow Inn. Now bear right to cross the East Bridge.

For the shorter walk, carry on up the road to reach a fork before a bend, and bear
right along Whitmead Lane to reach the entrance to 'Whitmead' itself. Continue along
the track outside the wall to reach The Donkey Inn. There, cross the main road (Charles

Hill) and walk along the track opposite for 30 yards to rejoin the longer walk.

The longer walk turns left at a telephone box, going along a bridleway. Turn left along the drive to go past Tilhill House. After 150 yards, go right at a fork and walk to the road by Sheephatch Farm. Cross and follow the bridleway to the foot of a gully and turn left along a sandy track to reach a road. Turn right for 200 yards, to the end of the wall of Keepers Cottage Stud. There, go left along a bridleway passing Yew Tree, Crooksbury, and the Waverley Cottages. At a road junction, turn left and walk to a car parking area. From the back of this climb up **Crooksbury Hill**. At the summit pillar, turn right, and, after a short descent, go left around the grounds of a large house. The track now swings left, keeping in the woods and becoming permissive bridleways P2, then 341. Follow these to reach a road. Turn right along Botany Hill into The Sands. At the crossing, turn right towards Cutmill, passing another Barley Mow Inn. About 150 yards beyond, turn right into Long Hill. A $1\frac{1}{4}$ mile (2km) straight track is now followed to reach some distinctive houses. Pass these and continue towards a main road and the Donkey Inn.

However, 30 yards before the road is reached, the long walk rejoins the short walk and turns left up a bridleway to join the drive of Amina Heights. Cross a road beyond the gatehouse and lodge to reach another path. At the end of this next path, another road is reached, by the entrance of Fullbrook Farm. Turn right, and just past the entrance to 'Brookfield', take the footpath going left. This soon reaches the bank of the Wey which is followed to a road. Turn left over the bridge to reach Elstead and the start of the walk.

POINTS OF INTEREST:

Tilford – A brief guide to Tilford village can be obtained for a small donation inside All Saints' church. The oak near the West Bridge is of very considerable age; read the plate affixed to the seat beneath it.

Crooksbury Hill – The pillar at the summit acknowledges the work of T V S Durrant, Surrey's Planning Officer 1951–1968. It was restored in 1991 as part of the bi-centenary celebrations of the Ordnance Survey and has a direction plate on top. Unfortunately, there is a restricted view due to tree growth, but the ruins of Waverley Abbey can just be seen. The abbey was the first Cistercian monastery built in England, having been founded in 1128.

REFRESHMENTS:

There are inns in both Elstead and Tilford.
The Barley Mow, The Sands.
The Donkey Inn, on the B3001, Charles Hill.

Walk 87 BEARE GREEN AND LEITH HILL TOWER   6m (9½km)

Maps: OS Sheets Landranger 187; Pathfinder 1226.

Visit both the highest inn and the highest point in Surrey!

Start: At 176437, Beare Green pond, near Holmwood station.

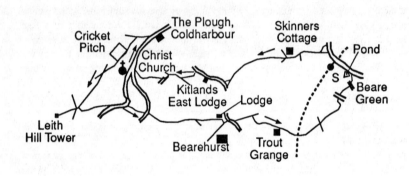

1 km

Walk up the road past the station, and take the footpath beyond the last house on the left. Continue to join a lane and proceed to 'Skinners Cottage'. There, take the bridleway ahead (with a No Through Road sign), ascending to pass Moorhurst Manor. The way becomes a stony path beyond a barrier of two tree trunks, rising to a fork between houses: go right to join a road. Follow the road around a bend to reach 'Kitlands East Lodge', and, 150 yards further on, look out for a footpath finger-post on the left before the yellow hydrant. Cross the stile, and another at the end of the field, to reach a gravel track. Follow this, passing Kitlands Cottage, and walking around the brick wall of Kitlands Court. Just beyond the sleeping policeman traffic hump in the dip, take the path going up to the right, climbing up to a gate under overhead lines. Continue on under a large oak tree to reach a metal gate. Go through into an alley and follow it to reach a point just below Christ Church, Coldharbour. Now take the Dorking road into the village to reach the Plough Inn. Turn sharp left uphill and, shortly, take a right fork to walk past a National Trust sign for Coldharbour Common and, on the left, a memento of the 16 October 1987 storm in the form of an inscribed bench seat. At the top of the main track , you reach the cricket pitch, in a setting that would be hard to improve upon – heather-fringed and totally encircled by trees.

Take the track to the left of the information board, going through the wooden barrier. Keep ahead at much the same level until you reach the green-topped post bearing the number 2. Now keep left to reach Post 1, then descend ahead to reach another barrier by 'The Dukes Warren' sign. **Leith Hill Tower** is now up ahead: after a visit, return to this junction to continue on the uphill track waymarked with a red arrowhead and the 'L-in-the-car' logo, to reach the Landslip car park.

Go left along the road for 50 yards to reach a bend, then keep ahead, passing the memorial seat to Frank Longhurst. Further down, fork left to reach another road. Cross, and at the end of the short grass path beyond the red six-bar gate, go down the left side of a field into a dip. Now make for the field's top right corner, where you enter the next field. Go over a stile in the bottom right corner of this field and walk towards the house whose roof can be seen ahead. Bear left at the next field entrance, following the yellow arrowhead, to reach a drive by a duck pond. Turn left to reach a road by Bearehurst Lodge and go across to reach the white gates of Trout Grange. Walk along to the end of the hedge-lined drive, where there is a pond on the left and, ahead, the entrance pillars to the house border a cattle grid. Turn left to reach a green gate and pass a tennis court. Exit the field in its bottom right corner and go across the railway lines. Proceed ahead, duly crossing a farm track. Now bear left at the far woodland to reach a stile. Go over this, cross a bridge and continue up a path to reach Highland Road. Go straight ahead and then along the alley at the end of Woodside Road to reach Beare Green Court. The pond where the walk started is just along the road to the left.

POINTS OF INTEREST:

Leith Hill Tower – Leith Hill is the highest point in south-east England at 965 feet (294 metres). The tower was built by Richard Hull in 1766, and he is actually buried underneath it! The structure, which raises you to 1029 feet, was presented to the National Trust in October 1923 by a Reigate resident, Mr W J MacAndrew.

REFRESHMENTS:

The Plough Inn, Coldharbour.
Copperfield's Coffee Shop, in Beare Green Court.
Refreshments are also available at Leith Hill Tower, when it is open (see Walk 76).

Walk 88 WEYBRIDGE AND WALTON ON THAMES $6^1/_4$m ($9^1/_2$km)

Maps: OS Sheets Landranger 176; Pathfinder 1190.

A riverside walk all the way.

Start: At 068647, Town Lock, Addlestone Road, Weybridge.

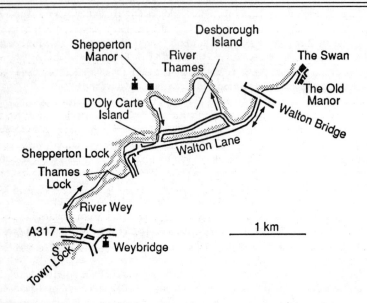

The two walks from Weybridge both commence at Town Lock, which is a short distance down Bridge Road from its junction at the end of Church Street (see Walk 25 for the other).

To start this walk, cross both bridges, over the river and navigation, and immediately turn right on to the towpath beside the River Wey. In just over $^1/_2$ mile, Thames Lock is reached, the last lock before the River Thames. Cross the bridge, leaving National Trust land and go along a concrete path. Go over a drive and pass to the right of a battery of garages. Beyond a bridge, turn left along Church Walk, continuing through the barriers and going past some very picturesque cottages.

At the Old Crown Inn, turn left along Thames Street, walking to the bend at the start of Walton Lane. Now go through a parking area, taking a look across to Shepperton Lock. The route soon reaches the steps which are the starting point for the foot ferry to Shepperton. It departs hourly or half-hourly depending on time and day, and is summoned by a long and hard ring on the bell!

Next, the route reaches the bridge across to the private **D'Oyly Carte Island**, beyond which is the start of the Desborough Channel. The return route will bring you down the steps of the bridge, but for now, pass underneath both this, and the similar bridge at the other end of the channel, about 1,100 yards (1,000 metres) distant. The path curls round through the Cowey Sale picnic area with its seats and weeping willows, and then passes under Walton Bridge, still looking temporary after many years!

Having gone over the plank bridge beyond Walton Marina, the walk reaches the moorings at Walton Wharf. Turn right, and right again at the top to see **the Old Manor House** located behind the inn of the same name.

Retrace the route to the bridge at this end of the channel, and go up the steps, turning right over the water. Follow the road down to the bend, then keep ahead along the gated drive to Brownacres. When the drive bears left, continue ahead on the narrow path, following the course of the river, which is often visible through the trees. Skirt Point Meadow to reach a bend from where the white mansion which is Shepperton Manor can be admired. There is also a mini-beach where toes could be dabbled while resting and looking across to the church tower behind the tree, and boathouse beside Warren Lodge Hotel.

Soon after the mini-beach the road is rejoined and the other bridge is crossed, this one bearing a panel commemorating the opening of the Desborough Channel in 1935. Descend the steps to reach the outward route and retrace your steps to regain the start.

POINTS OF INTEREST:

D'Oyly Carte Island – The island recalls Richard D'Oyly Carte, the producer of the Savoy operas of Gilbert and Sullivan. This was his summer residence.

The Old Manor House, Walton on Thames – This is a two-storey, timber-framed, grade 1 listed building, dating from the fourteenth century.

REFRESHMENTS:

The Queens Head, Weybridge.
The Old Crown, Weybridge.
The Lincoln Arms, Weybridge.
The Anglers Tavern, Walton on Thames.
The Swan, Walton on Thames.
The Old Manor Inn, Walton on Thames.

Walk 89   WESTCOTT TO FRIDAY STREET   6¹/₄m (10km)

Maps: OS Sheets Landranger 187; Pathfinder 1226.

A delightful walk along leafy by-ways.

Start: At 142486, Westcott village green.

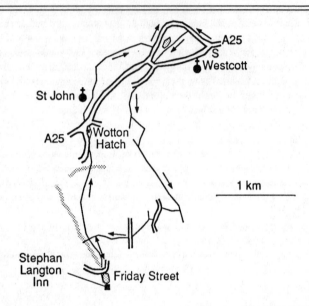

From the green, walk down Westcott Street to the junction with Springfield Road, then take the path going left beside Fir Cones. The path skirts a lake and some back gardens before reaching the A25. Cross with care and go along Rookery Drive opposite, passing Mill House and two other delightful cottages with a stream flowing between them. Continue along the track, which veers left below a row of town-houses and then starts to ascend. At a fork, keep left and continue along the bridleway to reach a T-junction at the end of a cutting, where you turn left.

After ¹/₂ mile, at the end of the last field on the right, go down right, keeping the wooded slope on your left. There is a barrier at the bottom beyond which the route goes left for 100 yards to reach a stile on the right, just past a gate.

Go over the stile and cross the grassland before climbing up a steep slope to reach a minor road. Cross and continue in the same direction for ¹/₄ mile, passing between sections of the Wotton Estate (private), to reach a descent beside wire fencing. At the bottom of the descent you will be facing a bridge between two lakes, with a charming house nestling among the trees.

The route continues by going right, over the stile, but to see **Friday Street** with its picturesque lake, turn left, and bear right at Yew Tree Cottage. The **Stephan Langton** Inn is a short way beyond the head of the lake.

If you have visited Friday Street, retrace your steps and go over the stile to enjoy one of the most picturesque parts of the walk, where a series of small lakes can be glimpsed through the holly bushes on your left. At a path fork, bear right uphill. Descend to cross a meadow with the Tillingbourne flowing through it. Enter a field beyond the copse on the far side and head for the opposite corner to reach a car park and Wotton Hatch restaurant.

Cross the road and walk down the lane, towards the church of St John the Evangelist, for 75 yards to reach a stile on the right. Go over into a field and make your way down the middle of a little valley. At the bottom, cross another stile to reach a lane with a cluster of buildings and a letter box. Turn right along the track, which later becomes surfaced, to reach a T-junction, with the spire of Westcott church just visible ahead. Turn left, and after crossing the bridge beyond the pink-painted Old Mill House, return up Westcott Street to the village green.

POINTS OF INTEREST:
Friday Street – The pond here was created by damming one of the streams feeding the Tillingbourne, originally for the purpose of driving a mill.
Stephan Langton – The inn is named after an Archbishop of Canterbury who was instrumental in forcing King John to sign the Magna Carta in 1215.

REFRESHMENTS:
The Crown Inn, Westcott.
The Prince of Wales, Westcott.
The Cricketers Inn, Westcott.
The Stephan Langton Inn, Friday Street.
Wotton Hatch Restaurant, on the A25.

Walk 90 MICKLEHAM, BOXHILL AND DENBIES VINEYARD 6¼m (10km)

Maps: OS Sheets Landranger 187; pathfinder 1206.

A climb to probably the most frequented viewpoint in Surrey, followed by a visit to Britain's largest vineyard.

Start: At 168518, Boxhill station.

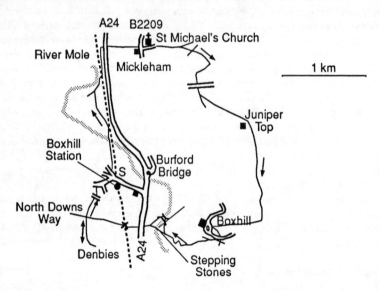

From the station, turn left over the bridge, then right down a path to a field. At the far end of the field, cross the River Mole and, ignoring the path under the arch, make for a house. Join a track and, in 150 yards, turn right to go under the railway to reach the main road. Cross both carriageways and continue along Swanworth Lane to reach Mickleham village.

Turn right, then left at the lych gate of St Michael's church, going along the drive to Eastfield Cottage. Beside the white gates, cross a stile and follow a path uphill. After forking right, the gradient increases: go ahead over a broad track, with the 'Mickleham Downs' sign to your left. Climb to the top of the ridge and descend slightly right. At the second iron stanchion, bear right to find a seat, from where you

172

can look ahead to Leith Hill on the distant skyline. Continue down the path, with the church spire of St Barnabas on Ranmore Common ahead. After 200 yards there is a steep descent, aided in the lower stages by over 120 steps.

Cross the road and go up the track opposite to find a map of the Boxhill area affixed to a bole. Take the path on the left after 25 yards and climb to Juniper Top. From here, you can look back to Norbury Park House and, 90 degrees to the right, the spire of Headley church. Enter the woodland along the lower path to find a green metal gate. Go through this to enjoy a level mile walking to reach a compound. Follow the track for 100 yards past this to reach a clearing, then go ahead on a grassy path to reach the Donkey Green and, beyond, the Boxhill National Trust Information Centre and Tea Rooms.

Locate **the viewing platform**, and take the path in the direction of Hindhead. This is the North Downs Way, marked with the acorn logo of National Trails. Just beyond the end of the grass slope, turn left at a post and descend to cross the River Mole by the stepping stones. The new bridge downstream, built in 1992, is recommended for the nervous or if the water level is too high.

Continue up to, and across, the A24, staying on the North Downs Way, which is just over to the left. Go through a railway arch and enter the **Denbies Wine Estate**. After 400 yards there is a crossing: turn left through the vineyard to visit the Winery and Visitor Centre; turn right to return to the station, crossing one road and going right at the second, Chapel Lane.

POINTS OF INTEREST:

The viewing platform – with its direction plate, commemorates the gift of Boxhill to the nation in 1914 by Leopold Salomons. He lived in Norbury Park House, which was seen from Juniper Top.

Denbies Wine Estate – This is England's largest vineyard, covering 250 acres. Over 275,000 vines are planted, with 20 grape varieties, producing mainly white wines. The chalk soil here is of the same composition as in the Champagne region of France! In the new Visitor Centre, hi-tech tours are available, with an audio-visual display. Visitors also visit the vaulted cellars where three wines may be sampled. Tel: 0306 876616.

REFRESHMENTS:

The Running Horses, Mickleham.

Tea, coffee and snacks are available beside Boxhill Information Centre.

Wine Tasting at Denbies.

The Stepping Stones Inn, between Boxhill station and A24.

Walk 91 NEWLANDS CORNER AND ST MARTHA'S $6^1/_4$m (10km)

Maps: OS Sheets Landranger 186; Pathfinder 1226.

Views, industrial history in the form of an old gunpowder factory, and some hill climbing.

Start: At 044493, Newlands Corner car park.

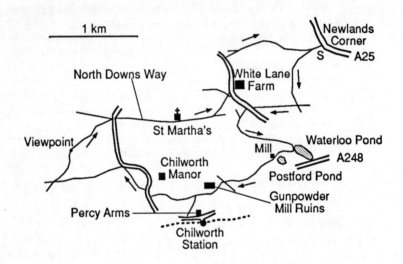

From the Countryside Centre, walk down the grass slope opposite to join a path veering right between two posts. After 20 yards, immediately past the first clump of trees, go off left down the hillside. Cross a track, and take the path through the copse ahead. Continue down the middle of a field to reach the buildings at the bottom. Pass to the right of the house and, 100 yards along the track, turn right to reach a road. Go across, along the sandy entrance to a car parking area, and then continue on a level grassy path beyond the St Martha's information board. The path soon drops downhill and a delightful stroll under deciduous trees ensues, with the Tillingbourne flowing at the base of the slope. The path reaches a house: do walk clockwise all around the pond, before continuing along the drive, going past another pond to reach the mill, at one time a trout farm. Cross a bridge over a sluice and turn right along a footpath beside a

174

field. Now go over four stiles to reach a lane. Cross the bridge ahead and immediately turn left along the bank going past a pipe. You will soon pass the ruins of an old **gunpowder factory**: about 200 yards later a fork is reached. For refreshment, turn left over the footbridge and, on reaching a road, go left to reach the Percy Arms, opposite Chilworth station. This detour to the inn adds $\frac{1}{2}$ mile to the walk.

If you have visited the inn, return to the fork and continue along the path, passing a row of millstones. An information board about the Chilworth gunpowder factory is situated just before you reach a road (Blacksmith Lane). Turn right along the road and, at the bend, go left, and at once fork right up a path alongside concrete posts. At the top, turn left and enter the field by the post box. Walk along the field's lower side, passing a barn in the dip. At the foot of the following rise, go right, over a stile, and up through the field beyond to reach another stile. Go over, and climb steeply to a rounded hilltop from where a fine view is obtained. Go forward to reach the edge of woods, and turn right along a grassy path. Walk past a camp site, and then descend to meet a road beyond a metal gate. Turn left along the road for 20 yards, then follow the North Downs Way, on the right, to reach the top of St Martha's Hill.

Beyond the **church**, a sandy track takes you downhill. Following the North Downs Way acorn logos, bear left to reach a road. Continue ahead on the path beside White Lane, going past the farm. A little way up the hill, cross the road, and return to Newlands Corner by walking across open downland.

POINTS OF INTEREST:

Gunpowder Factory – The ruined building and millstones along the bank are all that remain of Chilworth's gunpowder industry which flourished from the early 17th century until 1920. Finally, closure followed a fire that destroyed the mill. Previously, other explosions, some fatal, had rocked the area, including one that damaged St Martha's church.

St Martha's Church – The church tops the hill above the old Pilgrims' Way from Winchester to Canterbury. The church as it is today, dates from a restoration, completed in 1850, by Henry Woodyer, who was responsible for other church restorations in the area. A place of worship has, however, stood on this site for over a thousand years, and the present church was probably built around 1100, with masonry dating from a century later still visible today. In the churchyard is the grave of Yvonne Arnaud, who died in 1958, whose name is perpetuated in the name of Guildford's theatre.

REFRESHMENTS:

There is a café at Newlands Corner at the start of the walk.

The Percy Arms, opposite Chilworth station.

Walk 92   HASLEMERE AND BLACKDOWN   6½m (10½km)

Maps: OS Sheets Landranger 186; Pathfinder 1245 and 1266.

A hilly cross-border venture into West Sussex.

Start: At 904328, Haslemere Town Hall in High Street.

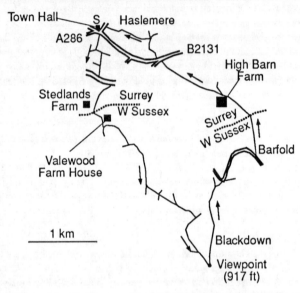

From the back of the red-brick Town Hall, go up College Hill, beside Barclays Bank. At the top, turn left along Hill Road, then right up Old Haslemere Road. At the T-junction, go left along Scotland Lane for about 150 yards, then, just before you come to Denbigh Road, turn right down the track between 'Littlecote' and 'Scarlets'. At the bottom is Stedlands Farm: turn left across the stream and enter West Sussex.

The route now follows the Sussex Border Path (SBP), established in 1989. Walk through the white gates and past Valewood Farm House. About 100 yards past this, turn left up the track. Just around the bend, turn right up the hillside, then go right at the top.

At the far end of the next field, turn left to reach a gate. Go through and walk uphill, shaded by rhododendrons. The clearly-marked path forks right and enters deciduous woodland. At the next fork go up left. Bear right at the top and then go

straight over at a crossing. Keep ahead until you come to a T-junction with a finger-post ahead in a triangle of grass, then go right, leaving the SBP for a while, to reach the edge of woodland. Here there are three memorial seats (one down to the right among the heather and bracken) from which you have a fine view to the west, followed later by two more, 200 yards apart.

You soon approach the top of Blackdown, at 917 feet. The view from the direction stone would be hard to better anywhere in the Home Counties. Keep the scarp slope on your right as you walk back along another wide woodland track to rejoin the SBP. Just before the car parking area, near the pillar for donations to the National Trust, take the path on the right which leads to a road. Now walk downhill, leaving the SBP.

In under $^1/_2$ mile (800 metres), at 'Barfold', turn left through a gate and go along a grass avenue beside the orchard to reach a stile. Go over and continue ahead to reach High Barn Farm. Bear half-left down the field to enter Barfold Copse, an RSPB Reserve. The track and roadway beyond lead to the busy B2131. Cross the road and go left to the end of the grassy bank beyond 'Merrymead'. There, take the footpath which drops down and turns right alongside a fenced field.

Walk to a junction beside the National Trust sign for Witley Copse and Mariners Rewe. The return into Haslemere from here is across the stream on the railed bridge and then through two fields to a drive. Continue ahead, passing a barn over to the left. Just around a left bend, go through a barrier on the right and cross the grass. Beyond the other barrier, go up the five steps and through the car park to return to the High Street.

POINTS OF INTEREST:
Blackdown – The long stone seat at the main viewpoint on Blackdown is in memory of Mabel Elisabeth, the wife of E W Hunter, who gave this area to the National Trust in 1944.

REFRESHMENTS:
None en route, but there is a choice in Haslemere.

Walk 93 THE DOWNS LINK PATH AND WONERSH 6¹/₂m (10¹/₂km)
Maps: OS Sheets Landranger 186; Pathfinder 1226.
A walk along the path which links the North and South Downs.
Start: At 031472, Chilworth Station.

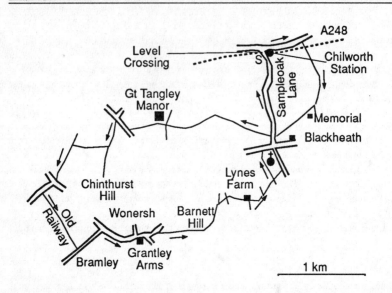

From the station, go along the A248 towards Dorking for ¹/₄ mile, passing a duck pond, and turn right by the bus shelter to join the **Downs Link Path**. This path is now followed as far as Bramley, navigation made easy by the finger-posts and logos.

Beyond the railway bridge, go ahead, and in under ¹/₂ mile reach a drive. Cross half-right and proceed through the woods. To the left of a clearing there is a memorial cross from where you have a clear view up to St Martha's church. The path turns left on to a track and crosses a road: the sign for Blackheath is just on the left. Continue ahead and pass Great Tangley Manor House. Cross a road and then go anti-clockwise around the base of Chinthurst Hill before reaching a road close to 'Southlands'.

Go ahead along Tannery Lane, and turn down left just before the bridge. You will notice that a smaller bridge nestles beside the one carrying the road: go over this and down to the track of an old railway. Turn left to reach Bramley and Wonersh

Station: the platform and nameboard still remain, and an information board about the Downs Link Path has been added.

At the road beyond, leave the Downs Link Path and turn left. Cross the stream on a new bridge and follow the road to the right into Wonersh. At the Grantley Arms, keep ahead towards Shamley Green, and then go along Barnett Lane.

A few yards past Woodyers Close, turn right on a gravel drive towards a metal gate and climb the path up Barnett Hill. At the top walk past the house, a Red Cross Training and Conference Centre. About 75 yards further on, fork right off the drive. Beyond the stile, walk ahead, passing the gravelled entrance to the Wonersh and Blackheath cemetery.

The narrow path drops down to skirt the barn and house of Lynes Farm, then ascends under the trees. At the junction by a blue ground-level 307 marker post, climb steeply right on an improved track to emerge at the top on to heathland. At the end of an enclosure of conifers, turn left, following a series of green arrowheads to reach Blackheath village beside St Martin's church. Turn right to the crossroads, then go left along Sampleoak Lane for nearly $^3/_4$ mile to return to the station.

POINTS OF INTEREST:
The Downs Link Path – This starts near St Martha's church on the North Downs Way and extends for 33 miles to reach the South Downs Way near Botolphs, north of Shoreham. From Bramley, it mainly follows the course of an old railway closed under the Beeching plan in the mid-sixties.

The smaller of the side-by-side bridges outside Bramley, spanned the Wey and Arun Canal, whilst the larger carried the road over the railway. The canal was completed in 1816, providing a link between the Thames and the South Coast, but closed in 1868.

REFRESHMENTS:
The Grantley Arms, Wonersh.
The Villagers, Blackheath (keep ahead at the crossroads).
The Percy Arms, opposite Chilworth station.

Maps: OS sheets Landranger 186; Pathfinder 1245 and 1266.
A long, but otherwise undemanding walk.
Start: At 960354, St Mary's Church, Chiddingfold.

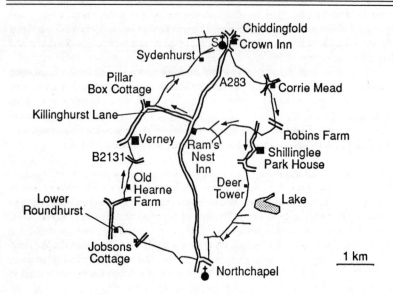

Go down the main road and cross a bridge. Just past Turners Mead, turn left up a path.
Beyond the gardens, cross a stile, walk ahead and bear slightly right and descend. Go
over a stile into woodland, at the top of which go left around a field. Re-enter the
wood in the corner and go down steps to a lake. Cross grassland to reach a gate
serving two fields. Go through and walk with the hedgerow on your right. In the far
corner, cross a stile and go down the drive of 'Old Pickhurst' to a road. Turn right.
Beyond 'Corrie Mead', go left and cross six fields, linked by stiles, to reach Robins
Farm. Go past the stables, then follow a horse track clockwise and walk to where
overhead lines clip the edge of a wood. Go over the poles and walk uphill. At the top,
across the grass, is a golf course: turn right along its edge to meet a road by Garden
Cottage.

For the shorter walk, take the path opposite. Go through a gate and keep left across a field. In the far corner of a second field, go through the gate beneath an oak tree. Now walk with the hedgerow on your left. A gate gives access to a wood, where you soon reach a crossing. Turn right, to reach a surfaced track serving Gostrode Farm. Turn left to reach the A283. The Ram's Nest is on the left. Continue the walk by going 150 yards right and then along Killinghurst Lane. After $^3/_4$ mile, at a left bend, rejoin the long walk by turning right along a finger-posted path.

For the longer walk, turn left along the road to reach a junction. Go left and, at a bend, keep ahead over a cattle grid. At a fork, go right, just below an avenue of trees. Pass to the left of Deer Tower and descend to the right corner of a field. Beyond a gate, you cross a bridge to a path that skirts a field and passes through a gap. Bear right uphill to reach a gate. Continue up to, and around, a house and walk beside a wall. At the T-junction at the far end of a long drive, turn right and after 50 yards fork half-left. Bear left again, just before a descent, to reach Northchapel. Cross the road and take the path beside Central House. Walk across fields and at a T-junction, turn right up a track to Upper Diddlesfold Farm. Keep ahead beside a barn, then go right into a field and aim for a wood. Cross a stile, and then another just around a left bend, to reach Jobson's Cottage. Go up the bank to the right and climb a field. Go into a field on the left at a gate and walk up to a track. Turn right. The track curves towards Lower Roundhurst: at the tennis court, go over a stile and up to a road. Turn right to reach a junction, then descend by bearing right. At the entrance to Old Hearne Farm, take the path parallel with the drive and walk past the house. Go through two gates and then go up past Anstead Brook Stud to reach the main road. Take the path opposite, going around a field towards the house in the distance. There, turn left to reach a road. Go right to pass the entrance to Furnace Place. Beyond parkland on the right, there is a road junction by Pillar Box Cottage: keep ahead.

At the first bend in the road, you rejoin the short walk: go ahead on to the path. Just before a gate, take a path on the left. Drop down to cross a stream on a footbridge. Half-way up the slope beyond, bear right to reach a bridleway. Go right and continue when it becomes an unmade road at the entrance to Hollyhurst. At Little Sydenhurst, turn left along the drive. Go to the left of a garage, then fork right to skirt a lake. At the top of a rise, cross a stile and aim half-right. Beyond two more stiles, the path reaches a residential road. At the end of the road descend to reach the start.

REFRESHMENTS:
The Ram's Nest, Ramsnest Common (shorter walk).
The Deepwell Inn, Northchapel (full walk).
The Crown Inn, Chiddingfold.

Walk 96   HYDON'S BALL AND ENTON   6¾m (10¾km)

Maps: OS Sheets Landranger 186; Pathfinder 1225 and 1245.
Lakes, and the charming cluster of buildings around the mill pond at Enton, give this walk a refreshing appeal.
Start: At 954414, Milford Station.

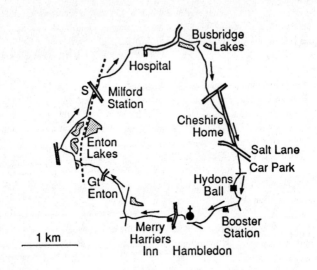

Leaving the station car park, turn left over the level crossing, then immediately left along a roadway parallel with the railway line. The road becomes a track, then veers right towards a house. Continue straight ahead past this, ignoring a path to the right. In 25 yards, cross a stream and proceed uphill. Skirt the grounds of Milford Hospital to reach a road at the hospital entrance.

Turn left down the hill and continue along the road to reach a sharp left bend. About 25 yards past this, at the end of a wire fence, take the footpath up right, and walk along the side of the lake. At its end, pass a barrier and turn right. The path soon climbs to join a field, with Busbridge Hall over to the left.

Continue along to meet a track and go past the houses to reach a road. Cross over on to a drive and veer left after 100 yards on to a bridleway which ascends gently to meet a road at the entrance to some nurseries. Turn right, passing the Hydon Hill Cheshire Home. In 400 yards, you will reach a road junction. Cross over to reach a National Trust sign and walk up the track, passing a car park on the left.

You meet a crossing track after 250 yards: look out for a cairn. Turn right here and at once go half-left to climb to the top of **Hydon's Ball**, at 586 ft. To descend, take the path just to the left of the triangulation pillar. This drops down to meet the base track by another National Trust sign. Turn right along the sandy track to pass the Thames Water Booster Station on your left, then continue across fields to reach St Peter's Church, **Hambledon**.

Beyond the church, by the wall of Stable Cottage, take the footpath on the right and drop down to the Merry Harriers Inn. Take the bridleway running along the right boundary of the inn. Just beyond where a two-plank bridge gets you over a muddy area, fork right. At a T-junction by an electricity pole, go right, following the line of poles. You soon enter a field, with Enton Hall over to the left. Just past a small lake, aim slightly left. Continue to the brow of a hill and go into the next field. There, go down half-left to reach a stile by a holly hedge. Go over on to a path and follow it to reach a road.

Go straight across to Great Enton. At the junction beyond the long barn, turn left. Go under a railway line to reach charming cottages facing a mill pond. Continue along the lane to reach a large brick building within sight of the main road. Turn right immediately beyond this, going down a footpath and then keeping ahead down a track and along the path beside the railway to arrive back at Milford station.

POINTS OF INTEREST:

Hydon's Ball – The seat on the top commemorates Octavia Hill, 1838-1912, one of the founders of the National Trust.

Hambledon – Opposite the wall of Hambledon churchyard, look out for the carved stone located above an ancient lime kiln, which was in use until the 19th century.

REFRESHMENTS:

The Merry Harriers Inn, Hambledon.

Walk 97   HOLMWOOD AND COLDHARBOUR   6³/₄m (10³/₄km)
Maps: OS Sheets Landranger 187; Pathfinder 1226.
The central section of this walk passes through glorious woodland.
Start: At 169472, St John's Church, North Holmwood.

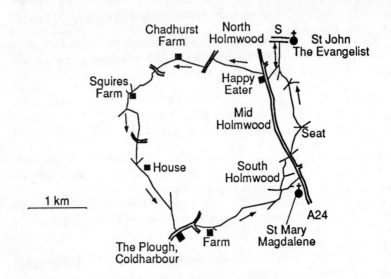

From the side of the church, take the path leading away from the village and go through a barrier into woodland. When you reach a clearing, veer half-right and pass through another barrier. Bear left, and then fork right after 50 yards to drop down to the A24. Cross over, with care, and turn right. About 50 yards past the Happy Eater motorist's restaurant, go up 16 steps and over a stile. Go forward to cross a bridge and then head in the general direction of a line of poles, towards a red-brick house.

Turn left along a road for 150 yards, then go right to Chadhurst Farm. Beyond the farmhouse and pond, walk ahead between the outbuildings and go through a metal gate. Once over the crest of the hill beyond, you will find two more gates and stiles leading to a road. Cross the road and proceed along the drive to Squires Farm. Go past the house, then go left on a sandy path, skirting the lawn to enter a forest.

At a path fork, go left and stroll through delightful woodland to reach a gravel crossing track. Here, go ahead up a steeper section of path, and at the top, bear right, then turn left to pass an isolated house. Continue along this sandy bridleway to reach Coldharbour at the Plough Inn.

Go left along the road to a junction, from where there is a fine view to Ranmore church. Turn right by White Cottage, and at the top of a rise, turn left down a concrete drive. Keep ahead between the barns, with the farmhouse over to the right and then stay on a grass path, ignoring the stile to the right. Your descent brings you to brick gate pillars at 'Taresmocks'; go over the stile just down to the left and continue alongside the wall.

At the bottom, leave the woodland and walk along the side of a field to exit in its right corner. Turn left along the roadway, with the tower of St Mary Magdalene ahead. At the junction just above the pastel-painted Betchets Green Farm, turn sharp left, then take the footpath to the right when you are under the trees. Cross a bridge and stile and walk along the bottom of a field to reach a road.

Walk to the other end of Warwick Close and turn right beyond the barrier to cross the A24. (If you use the subway, as you should, for safety's sake, return to the point directly opposite.)

Take the main grassy path half-left, entering Holmwood Common. Several paths criss-cross here, but they generally head in a northerly direction within earshot of the traffic. Follow one of these to reach an open area and viewpoint, with a bench-seat under a tree. From there, take the swathe sloping down half-left in the direction of the two tower blocks. This becomes a sandy track which winds through the woodland and, at length, it is joined by a broad gravel track from the right. Just after this the track swings left. Do not follow it: instead, look for the path under the oak at the back of the small triangular clump of trees. This rises to reach the open ground passed on the outward route. From there, retrace your steps back to the church.

POINTS OF INTEREST:
Holmwood – The village is split into three: North, where this walk starts, Mid and South, where the church of St Mary Magdalene is well worth the quarter-mile extension. Holmwood station, however, is not in any of the three, but at Beare Green!

REFRESHMENTS:
The Plough Inn, Coldharbour.
This is the highest pub in south-east England.

Walk 98 WOLDINGHAM AND MARDEN PARK 6³/₄m (10³/₄km)

Maps: OS Sheets Landranger 187; Pathfinder 1207.

Quite a strenuous circuit, using some neglected paths which may well be overgrown and muddy.

Start: At 370560, St Paul's Church, Woldingham.

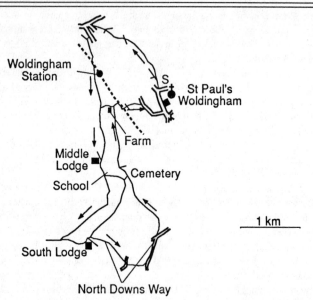

From the church, walk down Long Hill for 250 yards to a point just beyond the bungalow, 'Bramley Down'. Here fork half-right along a path between wire fences. Go past a seat to reach barriers. Turn left and immediately right along a bridleway. Cross a road at 'High Shaw' and walk downhill, going past an electricity enclosure. At the foot of the drive, turn left into Park Ley Road, bearing right after 25 yards to go down a path. At the bottom, turn left to reach the end of a brick wall and then cross a road to reach a bridleway. The bridleway meets the drive to **Woldingham School**: go left, under the railway arch, and walk past both the station and the entrance to Marden Park Farm, to enter the grounds at Middle Lodge, with its tall chimney. Go through the gate to reach a line of conifers fringing the red-brick main house. Just before the start of some wooden fencing on the right, climb a grass bank to reach a footpath marker-stone and enter woodland. The path bears left and gains height to emerge from the wood at a hillside. Continue between barbed wire fencing and, just beyond a tall concrete post at a wood barrier, follow the edge of the field on the left, continuing around a bulge in the wood. At the top corner, above the pole where electricity lines turn sharply downhill towards South Lodge (to be passed later), leave the field and continue in the direction of the fencing on the right. The path leads to another wood barrier at a right turn, and soon after you will start to descend. At the foot of some steps you join the North Downs Way: turn left past Winders Hill Cottages. Stay on the Way, going past South Lodge, and the road crossing at Hanging Wood Farm. After a descent almost to M25 level, walk up, or beside, a minor road to reach a T-junction at the top of the 14% hill. Go through the gap in front and keep ahead on a track, following a yellow arrowhead. You link up with a lower track: maintain direction around two deep hollows a short distance apart, then bear left along the top of a wide strip of grass. Turn right at a T-junction at the edge of a wood and continue to reach a stile giving access to a grassy slope. Follow a line of poles downhill and continue to reach a drive. Go forward around a cemetery, then fork left at a bend to go between hedges. By a metal gate, go straight ahead, walking parallel with the school drive used earlier. At Marden Park Farm, turn right just past the passage between the gabled barns to skirt a field. Half-way along the top side, cross a bridge over the railway and climb the hillside, passing between two trees. The long flight of steps beyond brings you to a residential road, Park View Road. Go forward to reach the green, then turn left along Station Road to the parade of shops and **St Paul's** church where the walk began.

POINTS OF INTEREST:

Woldingham School – Marden Park is the valley along which this walk passes. In 1672, a London banker, Sir Robert Clayton, bought the valley and built a country house, his heirs owning the estate until 1911. The original house was destroyed by fire in 1879, but the present building stands on the same site. The house and 700 acres of land were purchased in 1945 by the Society of the Sacred Heart, and Roehampton School, founded in 1842, moved here. It is now known as Woldingham School and is an independent girls' school with some 450 pupils, boarding and day.

St Paul's Church – The church was completed in 1933, as the successor to St Agatha's – thought to be Surrey's smallest church (not visited on the walk). On three sides of St Paul's tower is the inscription 'Praise Him and magnify Him forever'.

REFRESHMENTS:

None en route, but the village store passed near the end is useful for ice-creams etc.

Walk 99 RANMORE COMMON AND POLESDEN LACEY 8m (13km)

Maps: OS Sheets Landranger 187; Pathfinder 1206 and 1226.

A walk around Ranmore Common and along the North Downs Way.

Start: At 141503, the Denbies Hillside car park.

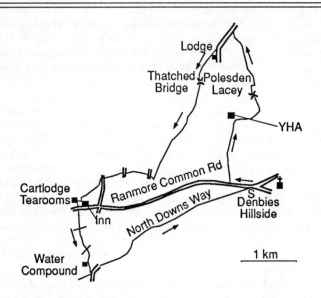

Walk west (away from the church) as far as the last house on the right, the one with the two prominent chimney stacks, and take the track to pass Tanner's Hatch Youth Hostel. Continue along the track, passing two metal gates in a dip, then climb up, ignoring a track off to the right. Pass under a bridge which carries a path into the grounds of **Polesden Lacey**, and continue for almost a mile to reach an approach road. Turn left to reach a fork. Go left here if you wish to enter Polesden Lacey grounds.

If you do not wish to visit the grounds, take the track towards Goldstone Farm from the fork. Beyond the house at the crest, pass under a thatched bridge, and at the end of the sloping wall, continue ahead down a yew-lined embankment. At a path junction, bear right up to Yew Tree Cottage. Continue on the main track for a further

150 yards to reach a gate on the right. Go through into a field and cross it keeping to the top side. In the second field, descend diagonally to cross a stile, and turn left up the track beyond.

Go past Pigden Cottage, and walk on to reach another house. Just beyond this, turn up right on to a track. Cross the road and continue along the track. After reading the memorial plate on the right, you descend on a holly-fringed path to join the drive leading from Haneys. Cross the road, taking the drive into Friars Elm for 100 yards. At a bend, go over the stile into the field ahead, exiting beside a metal gate and descending to a road.

Cross slightly to the right and take the path which climbs the bank, staying parallel with the road. Cross a stile out of the woodland and bear left around the field. Go through the green gate into the next field and then take the path between buildings to reach The Old Cartlodge Tearooms.

Walk up the drive to reach a road. Cross and take the path past Red Gables. At the path crossing, a permanent quagmire, go ahead and slightly left. Beyond another crossing, marked with white-banded posts, the path reaches a T-junction. Turn right to reach the East Surrey Water compound. (The triangulation pillar marked on the OS map is just beyond the enclosure.)

Turn left immediately before the railings on to a rutted track to emerge from the woodland. Descend through an area of forestry activity, going clockwise around a deep depression to meet the North Downs Way, marked with posts bearing an acorn logo. Turn left to reach a road.

Cross and return to the start by following this even, well-trodden – and, therefore, often muddy – National Trail. The route finding is very straightforward, and the views from the path are frequently excellent.

POINTS OF INTEREST:

Polesden Lacey – The grounds at Polesden Lacey are open daily from 11 am, but admission to the house itself is from April to October, Wednesday to Sunday, from 1.30 pm, and on Bank Holiday weekends (Sunday and Monday) from 11.30 am. Separate admission charges are made for the grounds and house. There is a restaurant and National Trust shop. The house was originally a Regency villa, but was remodelled after 1906 by the Hon Mrs Ronald Greville, a well-known society hostess. Tel: 0372 458203.

REFRESHMENTS:
The Old Cartlodge Tearooms.
The Ranmore Arms, Crocknorth Road.

Walk 100 BOOKHAM AND EFFINGHAM COMMONS $8\frac{1}{4}$m ($13\frac{1}{4}$km)

Maps: OS Sheets Landranger 187; Pathfinder 1206.

A level walk across the commons, with woodland and lakes as well.

Start: At 128556, Bookham station.

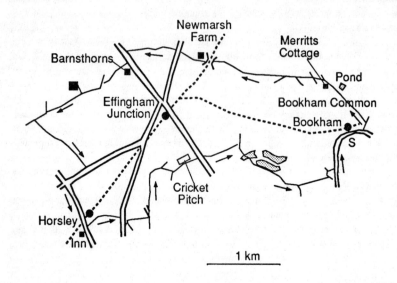

Leaving Bookham Station, turn left along the road to the bend. Go to the far end of the Commonside car parking area, where there is a National Trust information board and contribution pillar. Beyond this, take the bridleway to the left, which runs straight through woodland. In under ten minutes you pass a pond on the right and then come to Merritts Cottage.

Go forward for a few yards, then turn left opposite a small oak tree. Keep to the bridleway, going ahead at an offset crossing a couple of minutes later. Cross a stream on a concrete bridge and join a track to pass a couple of houses. Fork left, then right, to reach a stile. Go directly across the field ahead to reach another stile and bridge. At the end of the next field, aim for the railway arch in the distance. Beyond this, a track leads to a road. Go across and through a gate on to a path that goes through woodland to reach a crossing track beyond a large cleared area. Keep ahead and shortly join a track leading to another road.

Turn left for 175 yards, then go right at the sign for 'Barnsthorns'. When the drive veers left, cross the stile ahead. Go over a bridge and enter a field. Keeping to the right, walk into the next field and reach a path by a marker post. Turn left and pass a private drive going to a bungalow. Walk ahead along the path to reach a woodland track. Turn left and after 200 yards turn up left at a marker post. The path descends through a grove of rhododendrons to the edge of a field: go left to reach a road. Turn right to reach a junction. Go left and after the railway bridge, go up Horsley station approach as far as the cottage on the right. Take the surfaced path beside it.

Walk up through a gate to a green. Keep ahead along the road to reach a gate at the far end. Cross slightly left into Norrels Drive and turn left after 100 yards, near the lodges with their tall twin chimneys. The path soon joins a road: follow it to its end, then continue along a path. Cross Heath View and walk down the left side of the field. Swing right at the bottom, skirting the woodland, and keep ahead at a fork, going away from the trees with the hedgerow on your left. In the corner at the end of the hedgerow, go forward for 50 yards, then turn left along a stony track. Go past a red brick house and the cricket pitch to reach the main road, opposite the entrance to Norwood Farm.

Turn right, then left along Lower Farm Road. At its end, cross a metal stile and turn right to drop down to, and cross, the lake. Enter a field beyond the gravel drive and aim diagonally left towards the wire fence bordering the water. Follow the fence around to a metal gate, beside which is a squeezer stile. Four more follow, then the path turns right and swings left around a thicket to reach a wide S-bend. Here take the left path and, after 250 yards, go over a stile and down the left side of the field beyond to reach a residential road. Turn left and walk around to the main road. Turn left to return to **Bookham** and the station.

POINTS OF INTEREST:

Bookham – Bookham Common covers an area of 452 acres. Over 500 species of flowering plants have been recorded here, as well as ferns, mosses, lichens and fungi.

REFRESHMENTS:

The Horsley Inn, opposite Horsley station approach.

TITLES IN THE SERIES